Utilitarianism & Situation Ethics

Teleological Ethics

Peter Baron

Published by Inducit Learning Ltd trading as pushmepress.com,

Pawlett House, West Street, Somerton,

Somerset TA11 7PS, United Kingdom

www.pushmepress.com

First published in 2013

ISBN: 978-1-909618-16-9

Links, reviews, news and revision materials available on

www.philosophicalinvestigations.co.uk

With over 20,000 visitors a month, the philosophical investigations website allows students and teachers to explore Philosophy of Religion and Ethics through handouts, film clips, presentations, case studies, extracts, games and academic articles.

Pitched just right, and so much more than a text book, here is a place to engage with critical reflection whatever your level. Marked student essays are also posted.

Contents

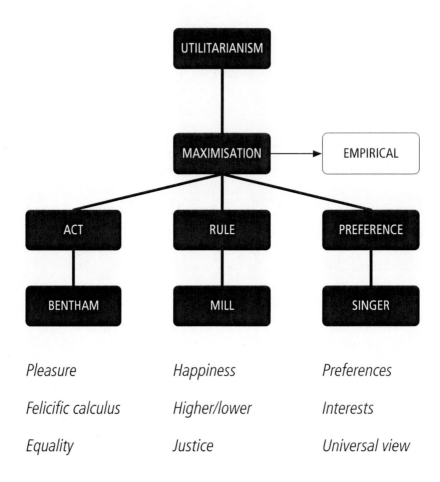

Pleasure	*Happiness*	*Preferences*
Felicific calculus	*Higher/lower*	*Interests*
Equality	*Justice*	*Universal view*

Teleological Ethics

Teleological ethics is the ethics of ends or purposes of actions (**TELOS** = end). What we ought to do (the right action) is based on the goodness of the end we aim for (the good). The motive for our action, the idea of law or duty so important to deontological ethics are things irrelevant to the idea of goodness. What matters is what we desire as the end. These theories are theories of the pursuit of rational desire - the ends that reasonable people really want.

ANALYSING

To analyse ethical theories we will ask four questions which spell the acronym **DARM**, which are then answered in the final chapter.

- **DERIVATION** - how is the idea of goodness derived? Where does it come from? What is the logic and line of reasoning? What assumptions are being made? What worldview forms the idea of good?

- **APPLICATION** - having decided where good comes from, how do we apply the idea to real world events and choices? What principles are involved? How do we think the theory through to produce a practical decision?

- **REALISM** - a theory can appear fine on paper, but how does it fit with our understanding of human nature? Does it makes sense to me, as someone who is supposed to reason about moral choices? Does it seem to correspond with what other disciplines such as psychology are suggesting? If not it may be better to discard the theory.

- **MOTIVATION** - a basic question we need to answer is: why should I be moral? Why should I care about my neighbour, or the starving in Africa? Why not just be an egoist, living for self and using others for my own ends?

How Teleology Works

Teleology identifies first the good we are aiming for. The idea of goodness differs in different teleological theories. But they generally share one way of calculating goodness: the assessment of consequences. Hence most teleological theories, and especially the theories in this book, are described as **CONSEQUENTIALIST**[1].

There are four ways the theories in this book describe this desirable aim.

- **PLEASURE** - Jeremy Bentham's hedonistic act utilitarianism.

- **HAPPINESS** - John Stuart Mill's eudaimonic (meaning happiness based, **EUDAIMONIA** is Greek for happiness) rule utilitarianism.

- **PREFERENCES** - Peter Singer's preference utilitarianism.

- **LOVE** - Joseph Fletcher's Situation Ethics.

So these theories seek to maximise in two senses: they seek to maximise a value (pleasure, happiness, love) for the maximum number of people. The aim of this book is to explore the theories, explain differences between them, and provide a thorough evaluation of their conclusions.

---

1 Virtue ethics is teleological but not consequentialist and Natural Law theory has teleological aspects.

AN EXAMPLE

An example will help bring out the essential difference between **DEONTOLOGICAL** (deon = duty) and **TELEOLOGICAL** ethics (telos = end). I promise to go to my friend's party on Saturday night. My friend is rather dull and humourless, and I think the party may be fairly boring. The next day another friend invites me to a rave on the same night. I sense this party will be really good fun. Taking the end of my happiness as the sole criterion for judging the rightness of my action, I break my promise to my other friend, miss her party and go to the rave.

The next day my disappointed friend arrives crestfallen. "You didn't make the party", she moans, in a pained way. "Sorry mate", I reply, "I was ill". I sense that she would be really upset if I told the truth, so I lie. I have made the calculation that by so acting, and then lying, happiness is maximised.

To the deontologist, Immanuel Kant, I have committed four wrongs.

1. I cannot universalise my action because I wouldn't want my friends to treat me like that.

2. I have broken a promise, and so undermined the general rule that promise-keeping is good.

3. I have acted out of the selfish motive of pleasure, not my duty to do the right thing.

4. I have used my first friend as a means to an end - I have broken my promise to her in order to go to the second party.

MY ACTIONS ALSO BEG SOME QUESTIONS

1. Why should happiness or pleasure be seen as the supreme good? Why not, as Kant argued, duty?

2. Whose happiness do I include in my calculation of which action is best? What weight do I put on the pain I am causing my first friend versus the pleasure I am causing my other friends?

3. What exactly do I mean by happiness? Is it the same as pleasure? Is happiness a state of contentment, a sort of mental equilibrium, or is it a sensation of excitement or pleasure?

4. Is it morally right to sacrifice one person's happiness to benefit the majority?

These questions give us the main issues surrounding utilitarian ethics, and explain why some people argue utilitarianism and other forms of teleological ethics discussed in this book have immoral outcomes.

TWO TYPES OF TELEOLOGY

Greek ethics - perfectionism

Greek ethics comes out of a teleological worldview, but it's important to notice that teleological ethics isn't always **CONSEQUENTIALIST**. Aristotle (384-322 BC) for example argued every thing or person had a function and the good is seen as the excellent performance of that function. Aristotle called this ultimate purpose the final cause. The final cause of a knife is to cut well, and the final cause of a human being is to reason well.

The Greeks emphasized the cultivation of virtue or excellence as the means to flourishing or **EUDAIMONIA**, where flourishing is the final end of all action. Eudaimonia is sometimes translated as happiness, but is in fact an organic idea which we grow into as we follow and cultivate the virtues or habits of excellence. The goal is perfection arrived at by developing appropriate habits, hence John Rawls calls this view "perfectionism". Rather than a psychological state like pleasure, eudaimonia is a state of character in which certain habits produce right judgment, and realise the true potential of the rational human being.

These habits could be the classical virtues such as courage, temperance, justice, and wisdom which produced the Greek ideal of man as the "rational animal"; or the Christian virtues such as faith, hope, and love that in Aquinas' thought (building on Aristotle's insights) mark the Christian ideal of humankind as created in the image of God. The ideal of the Christian is the moral perfection of Jesus Christ.

So to the Greeks, the only good-in-itself or intrinsic good is eudaimonia - personal and social flourishing as the final goal of all rational human action, a richer term than the pleasure-based view of happiness. But virtue ethics is a non-consequentialist moral theory as goodness is defined by character traits which cause us to flourish, rather than consequences assessed from any particular action.

The utilitarians - empiricism

Utilitarian ethics examines the goodness or badness of consequences (consequentialism). A consequence is good when it results in maximum happiness and bad when it produces unhappiness. Its chief proponents are Bentham (1789), Mill (1861) and Sidgwick (1907), and in the modern era, RM Hare and Peter Singer. The consequences can be calculated **EMPIRICALLY** (empiricism) to give a balance figure of good over bad, added up or aggregated for all those affected by a decision.

Utilitarians divide into two main types. **ACT** consequentialists argue that the goodness of an act depends on the good consequences measured as a balance of pleasure over pain, or with preference utilitarians, the maximisation of first preferences. We measure objectively the greatest happiness of the greatest number and choose the act which maximises net happiness - taken as a balance figure of positive pleasure minus negative pain. Those who emphasise pleasure are called hedonists - they see pleasure as the only intrinsic good. So Bentham is a hedonic act utilitarian.

RULE utilitarians such as Mill argue that some rules are necessary to protect our security and welfare, rules such as the right to a fair trial, or freedom of speech. We explore the difference between Bentham and Mill in the central section of this book. Rather than focus on an individual action, rule utilitarians place the stress on rules that generally promote happiness. The telos of happiness is given a **DEONTOLOGICAL** twist :

rules are a means to the general end or telos of happiness. Just exactly what are the function of rules in Mill's Utilitarianism is hotly debated. In this book I side with J.O.Urmson[2] who classifies Mill as a rule utilitarian.

---

2 J.O. Urmson The Interpretation of the Philosophy of J.S. Mill (1953)

Bentham's Hedonistic Act Utilitarianism

INTRODUCTION

Jeremy Bentham defined **UTILITY** as:

"That property which is any object, whereby it tends to produce benefit, advantage, pleasure, good, or happiness...if the community in general, then the happiness of the community; if a particular individual; then the happiness of that individual".

So, Utilitarian philosophers such as Bentham (1748-1832) and Mill (1806-1873) claim that their philosophy is useful for two reasons: it helps define what is good and it helps us make decisions on a personal level by examining the consequences of our choices, and on a collective level by giving us an indicator of **WELFARE** for society.

There are three general features of utilitarian philosophy that go with the consequentialism discussed in the previous chapter:

- **EMPIRICAL**

- **TELEOLOGICAL**

- **NATURALISTIC**

Utilitarianism is an empirical philosophy because it claims happiness or pleasure can be observed, calculated and applied to real-life situations. As Mill argues in Utilitarianism, "according to one opinion, the principles of morals are evidently a priori[3], requiring nothing to command assent, except that the meaning of their terms be understood. According to the other doctrine, right and wrong are questions of observation and experience" (Utilitarianism, 1.3). So utilitarianism is an **A POSTERIORI** theory of goodness, where a posteriori means coming "from experience".

Furthermore, Utilitarianism is teleological because the calculation concerns consequences, as discussed in the introduction, which result from pursuing the end or telos of pleasure or happiness in the fulfilment of rational desires.

And thirdly it is naturalistic because an "ought" is derived from an "is": what "is" the happiest state of affairs is the one we "ought" to create. "Goodness" becomes a property of something in the natural world which utilitarians believe we can measure, that something being pleasure (the **HEDONISTIC** utilitarians) or happiness (the **ACT** and **RULE** utilitarians) or preferences (the **PREFERENCE** utilitarians like Henry Sidgwick and Peter Singer).

BENTHAM'S HEDONISTIC ACT UTILITARIANISM

In the next two chapters we will consider and compare two classical utilitarians who emerged in an era of social reform and revolution: Jeremy Bentham and John Stuart Mill. Table 1 (page 55) summarises the major differences between them. Both were social reformers who placed measurable improvements in the welfare of human beings as central to their ethics.

---

3 Kant's is an a priori theory because Kant argues moral truths are derived from reason before experience.

Jeremy Bentham (1748–1832) is the father of modern Utilitarianism. From one principle he devised a complete ethical system which even embraced animals. He never thought that the aim of Utilitarianism was to explain ordinary moral views; it was, rather, to reform them. This one principle he calls the greatest happiness principle.

"By the principle of utility is meant that principle which approves or disapproves of every action whatsoever according to the tendency it appears to have to augment or diminish the happiness of the party whose interest is in question. I say of every action whatsoever, and therefore not only of every action of a private individual, but of every measure of government". (1789:2)

Some people have classified Bentham as an egoistic act utilitarian. But Bentham always emphasised the social and political aspects of human happiness. He campaigned for universal suffrage, equality for homosexuals, and even the abolition of the monarchy. He spent his whole working life producing a code of law and even designed a humane prison called a Panopticon. He was convinced that powerful interests were stopping ordinary people enjoying a better life. His thinking has been one of the foundations of our modern liberal state.

THE ONE INTRINSIC GOOD IS PLEASURE

Bentham begins his Principles of Morals and Legislation (1789) with an abrupt statement about intrinsic goodness: "Nature has placed mankind under the sovereign governance of two masters, pain and pleasure". There is only one thing that is good, and one bad, and those two things are both sensations that every human being shares. If we know anything, we at least know what pain and pleasure are.

Bentham shares with Thomas Hobbes a concern with what human beings tend to do. Whereas Hobbes reduces our motive to two desires: fear - the desire to run away, and aggressiveness, the desire to attack and accumulate, Bentham in his emphasis on pain and pleasure follows the Greek philosophers like Helvetius who argued "physical pain and pleasure are the unrecognised principles of all human actions".

Bentham argued that this psychological motive was present even when the person denied it and seemed to behave otherwise. So the ascetic who gives up worldly goods and sensations to live a life of self-denial is actually gaining pleasure from the self-denial (and the pleasure of status if society thinks asceticism is noble).

Whereas a natural law theorist sees good coming from the tendencies of a shared rational human nature, Bentham sees goodness in a shared experience. He explicitly rejects conscience, God, duty, or some ideal nature as the source of goodness. The standard of right and wrong is "fashioned upon the fact that pleasure attracts and pain repels".

From this starting point in psychological motivation (a fact or something given in human nature), Bentham develops a theory of morality which aims to "rear the fabric of felicity", in other words, produce the social and personal circumstances where pleasure is maximised and pain minimised. This becomes to Bentham the origin of a social and political programme of reform that embraced prisons, women's rights and the extension of democracy. Utility becomes the property in any object which makes it useful for promoting happiness and preventing pain. He later developed this into the greatest happiness principle.

MAXIMISING HAPPINESS

Bentham takes a psychological fact - that people pursue pleasure and avoid pain, and turns it into a normative principle (a general rule of conduct). According to Bentham, people embrace utilitarianism "by their natural constitution". But when applied to society, it is important to notice that Bentham does not believe in a higher concept of society. Community, he argues, is a fiction apart from its members.

The interest of society becomes "the sum of the interests of the several members who compose it". There are echoes here of Mrs Thatcher, who in 1987 declared "there is no such thing as society, just individuals"[4]. In Economics we have the idea of cost/benefit analysis. Before putting in a crash barrier we analyse how many lives could be saved. Often the crash barrier doesn't go in until some deaths have occurred. A human life is given a value, and then we compare the benefit of saved lives against the cost of putting in the barrier. The decision to put in the barrier conforms to the principle of utility when "the tendency it has to augment the happiness of the community is greater than any it has to diminish it" (II.5).

Notice we can apply Bentham's principle to all kinds of political decisions Should we have more wind farms? Should we build a high speed rail link

---

4 *Interview in Women's Own, September 1987*

between London and Birmingham? There will always be protesters arguing for negative effects (pains) of such policies, such as the noise of windfarms, their appearance, the effect on wildlife such as birds striking the turbines. It is the job of Government to add up benefits and costs and do the utilitarian thing - maximise the happiness of most people (whilst acknowledging and apologising for the negative effects and also ignoring vague statements about the beauty of the countryside which have no objective utilitarian basis).

From this empirical calculation we derive an important idea of equality. In adding up pleasure and subtracting pain, "everyone is to count for one, and no-one as more than one". It doesn't matter if you are a landowner on the new rail link, or whether you live in a village close by, or whether you are a Duke whose estate is to be affected by the high speed rail link. Everyone has equal chips when it comes to the utilitarian table, and my pleasure is of equal value to yours.

To David Brink, this fact that social happiness isn't quite the same as personal happiness entails a logical problem that renders Bentham's theory of utilitarianism false. "Indeed, utilitarianism appears false and not just irrelevant if we also assume the voluntarist principle that ought implies can".

1. **WHAT** maximizes human happiness (pleasure) does not always maximize the agent's own happiness (pleasure).

2. **OUGHT** implies can. What I should do implies I am able to do it.

3. So I should be able to maximise both my own happiness and everyone else's, but I find I can't.

4. Hence, I cannot have an obligation to maximize both individual

and social happiness (pleasure)".[5]

Is the first premise valid? If not, we have our first objection to utilitarian ethics.

5 David O. Brink internet resources

ALL PLEASURES (AS WELL AS PEOPLE) ARE EQUAL

There is a second idea of equality in Bentham. Not only is my pleasure of equal value to your pleasure in the utilitarian calculation, but there is no difference between the type of pleasure we are experiencing. Bentham argues that I can be a sadist, enjoying pleasure by inflicting pain, I can be cruel - as long as there are no adverse consequences, then the pleasure makes the action good. Bentham argued:

"Let a man's motive be ill-will, call it even malice, envy, cruelty; it is still a kind of pleasure that is his motive: the pleasure he takes at the thought of the pain which he sees, or expects to see, his adversary undergo. Now even this wretched pleasure, taken by itself, is good: it may be faint; it may be short: it must at any rate be impure: yet while it lasts, and before any bad consequences arrive, it is good as any other that is not more intense".

Moreover, there is no qualitative distinction between pleasures of the body and those of the mind. "Pushpin is as good as poetry", asserted Bentham. Pushpin was a pub game involving pushing a penny up a board. In today's language we'd say "playing computer games is as good as reading Ted Hughes". But are all pleasures actually of equal value? Is it of equal value that I read poetry or eat jelly snakes at 2p each?

Bentham concluded confidently that "Prejudice apart, the game of push-pin is of equal value with the arts and sciences of music and poetry. If the game of push-pin furnishes more pleasure, it is more valuable than either".

HOW DO WE MEASURE PLEASURE?

A central problem is how we measure pleasure or happiness, because it seems a subjective concept to ask how much pleasure out of ten you're getting from eating that Mars Bar. If sensuous pleasure is really of equal hedonic value to listening to Mozart, how are we going to measure and compare each?

Bentham believed that pleasures were empirically measurable by a felicific calculus. This calculus had seven dimensions which give the utility calculation a value in some measure (shall we call them utils?).

In estimating a pleasure by itself, Bentham asks us to consider four dimensions.

- **INTENSITY** - how strong is the pleasure?

- **DURATION** - how long does it last?

- **CERTAINTY** - how sure is the pleasure?

- **PROPINQUITY** - how near is it, or how soon will I experience it?

Henry Sidgwick criticises Bentham for placing such a value on propinquity. For the more distant a pleasure, the more uncertain may be its occurrence. Henry Sidgwick (1838-1900), a later British utilitarian, criticizes Bentham on precisely this point.

"Proximity is a property of pleasures and pains which it is reasonable to disregard except in so far as it diminishes uncertainty. For my feelings a year hence should be just as

important to me as my feelings next minute, if only I could make an equally sure forecast of them. Indeed this equal and impartial concern for all parts of one's conscious life is perhaps the most prominent element in the common notion of the rational – as opposed to the merely impulsive – pursuit of pleasure" (Methods of Ethics 124n; cf. 111).

Then Bentham asks us to consider whether the pleasure will lead on to further pleasures and suggests two more dimensions. These two result from actions.

- **FECUNDITY** - how many more pleasures will result?

- **PURITY** - are there any negative pains attached to the pleasure?

Then Bentham applies these to the wider group:

- **EXTENT** - how many more people are affected?

This produces the principle : act in such a way that your actions produce the greatest amount of pleasure and the least amount of pain.

However, a problem emerges which worried later utilitarians like Henry Sidgwick. Where this principle provides a motivation for my action, why should I care about the happiness of others? It is not clear why I should want to maximise the happiness of a stranger I'd never met, rather than just my family and friends. Moreover, do we need this complex list of seven dimensions?

David Brink suggests:

"The whole taxonomy seems unnecessarily complex. Because

the utilitarian asks us to maximize value, he has to be able to make sense of quantities or magnitudes of value or pleasure associated with different options, where pleasure increases the value of an option and pain decreases the value of the option. Intensity and duration are really the only two variables[6].

Suppose as a teacher I discover a colleague leaking exam questions to his students. If I blow the whistle and expose the fraud, my own career could be in ruins as I may be blacklisted by the school and other schools for rocking the boat. Moreover, my colleague's career will be ruined and his students will do less well and so their happiness will be less. So as an action it seems to be the right thing to keep quiet.

But the general happiness of society, including those students who will just fail to get in to the university of their choice because his students have done better than they should, seems to demand that I speak out. But why should I care about the wider society? After all, I will never meet them, whereas I will meet those gaining from the act of cheating every day.

It is hard to see how utilitarians would ever be whistle blowers.

---

6 David O Brink ibid.

THE LOGIC OF UTILITARIANISM

Here in outline is the logic of the utilitarian position. It's important to see that the utilitarians are trying to find an objective way of advancing social welfare and for judging between competing demands, for example, on a Government. This principle is called "the principle of utility" or the "greatest happiness principle".

1. There is an empirical (measurable) way to calculate goodness - goodness has an objective basis.

2. This objective basis is the maximisation of happiness - something is good if it maximises the greatest happiness of the greatest number.

3. There is a radical equality in this - whether you're the Queen or a homeless person, "everyone is to count for one and no-one more than one" (Bentham).

4. If a good act is one that maximises pleasure over pain, how do we measure pleasure?

5. Bentham (a hedonic act utilitarian) thought we could measure the hedons (pleasure units) we get from an action.

6. He calls this the hedonic calculus (acronym P.R.R.I.C.E.D. Purity Remoteness Richness Intensity Certainty Extent Duration).

7. The problem is - how do I know my hedon equals your hedon?

8. Mill objected to this idea - he thought his poetry hedon was worth more than your football hedon. So he argued for higher and lower pleasures, of the mind and body respectively.

9. He also worried about the majority voting to oppress (lynch) the minority.

10. Mill argues that rights and justice are necessary to guarantee a happy world - if we all have rights we'll be happier.

11. The problem of calculating pleasure hedons also meant it was easier to follow rules - which are the accumulated wisdom of everyone before you.

12. Except when two rules conflict - then we can make an act utilitarian calculation (conflicts are a problem for nearly all moral theories. Should I lie to save a friend's reputation?).

13. Singer's preference utilitarianism includes all feeling species in the calculation and seeks to maximise preferences and interests. (I argue here that Singer isn't very consistent on this and ends up arguing for preferences for superior beings and pleasure/pain calculation -by someone else - for inferior beings).

IMPLICATIONS OF BENTHAM'S HEDONISTIC UTILITARIANISM

One implication that Bentham failed to spot is that there is a difference between social needs and social happiness. This can be illustrated with an example.

Suppose as a Government I am faced with a choice, to locate a hospital in Northwood or Watford. The Government does a needs assessment that yields the following results in net utils (ie pleasure minus pain) by age group.

AGE GROUP	NUMBERS OF PEOPLE NORTHWOOD	NUMBERS OF PEOPLE WATFORD	HEDONS PER PERSON	TOTAL HEDONS
0-15	300	50	20	N 6000
				W 1000
16-40	100	250	5	N 500
				W 1250
40-60	50	100	20	N 1000
				W 2000
60-90	20	100	40	N 800
				W 4000
TOTAL	470	500		N 8300
				W 8250

The age group 60-90 have the most need - their utils are 40 per person from having a hospital nearby. Yet the decision would be, locate in

Northwood (total hedons 8300 compared with 8250 for Watford). This is because Northwood has a lot of people aged 16-40 who would get a very small gain from locating there. So on total utility grounds, Northwood wins.

But what about average utility? In terms of average utility I divide 8300 by 470 people and I get a measure of 17.67 utils per person. Whereas in Watford I count 8250 divided by 500 people, which is 16.50 per person. On this measure, Northwood also wins.

Yet the most needy, those who have an average utility score of 40 per person are the 60-90 year olds. They are the ones who will find it hardest to get to a hospital further away. They are the ones who will use it more. And there are only 20 of these living in Northwood, and 100 near the Watford site. Surely these most vulnerable people should gain more weight in the calculation? Where does need come in where we simply aggregate utility?

We can call this consequence of utilitarian ethics a version of the tyranny of the majority. Even when utils are added up, it is the most people who benefit not those with greatest need. Of course, in democracies we tend to consider a simple preference (preference utilitarianism) rather than the strength of pleasure and pain (hedonistic act utilitarianism). We do literally add up votes rather than measuring intensity of pleasure.

SMART'S PLEASURE MACHINE

Are all types of pleasure equally good? In Utilitarianism For and Against, JJC Smart asks us to consider a man who has electrodes inserted into his brain.

"This calls up a pleasant picture of the voluptary of the future, a bald-headed man with a number of electrodes protruding from his skull, one to give the physical pleasure of sex, one for eating, one for drinking, and so on. Now is this the sort of life our ethical planning should culminate in?" (1994:19).

Smart puts forward several objections to the balding sensualist (voluptary) in a permanent state of heightened pleasure. One is that such pleasures would be, to use Bentham's word in the felicific calculus, infecund - they would not lead on to other pleasures, indeed, the normal pleasures of life would be diminished by this experience, as we might give up normal life in favour of life on the machine. Certainly the pleasure of normal relationships, conversation, friendship would be impossible to the man plugged into the machine. Rather than leading on to more pleasures (as would happen, for example, by improving my skill of poetry writing or listening to music) the pleasure machine would make further pleasures of the non-electrode sort almost impossible.

Secondly, he argues that we would not want such a state if it was offered to us even if we recognise we might be quite happy when we're in it. It is analogous to the idea that an Alzheimer's victim might be quite happy in their state of being, but that I would prefer to have a living will requiring euthanasia should I ever find myself in that state. As I look forward I simply don't want that sort of happiness.

Smart concludes (and Mill would agree as we shall see shortly) that utilitarianism is not just a descriptive idea. There are good and bad states of happiness. Happiness is an evaluative concept. It seems that merely quantifying pleasure doesn't do justice to the idea that some pleasures are good and some, like being plugged into the pleasure machine, are bad. I need to be happy with the idea of happiness.

ANIMAL RIGHTS

Bentham was the first philosopher to argue that animals had rights. We do not consider animal pain and pleasure for cultural reasons and because we think they feel less pain than we do. It is their lack of power to negotiate a right and the arrogance of humans which, according to Bentham causes us to ignore their suffering.

> *"The day has been, I am sad to say in many places it is not yet past, in which the greater part of the species, under the denomination of slaves, have been treated by the law exactly upon the same footing, as, in England for example, the inferior races of animals are still. The day may come when the rest of the animal creation may acquire those rights....a full-grown horse or dog, is beyond comparison a more rational, as well as a more conversable animal, than an infant of a day or a week or even a month, old. But suppose the case were otherwise, what would it avail? The question is not, Can they reason? nor, Can they talk? but, Can they suffer? (1823: fn chapter 17)*

Animals are treated as our slaves, Bentham feels, despite the fact that we are just animals ourselves. Animals cannot make plans for the future even though some have self-awareness. However, it is okay to kill animals for food as long as they do not suffer pain, because "the fate that awaits them is not worse than the fate that awaits them in nature".

We should not cause animals suffering because they are conscious, sentient (feeling) beings. Bentham's argument can be presented as a syllogism (a logical form of argument where one thing follows from another):

1. Animals can feel pain.

2. Our actions can affect their welfare.

3. A good action involves taking into account all pain and pleasure.

4. Therefore the pain and pleasure of animals needs to be included in our calculation.

Is this enough? Martha Nussbaum argues that "Bentham's radical abhorrence of suffering and his admirable ambition to bring all sentient beings to a state of well-being obscured, for a time, the fact that well-being and satisfaction might not be all there is to human good, or even all there is to happiness. Other things, such as activity, loving, fullness of commitment - might also be involved". (Daedalus, vol 133 no 2 pp 60-68).

Mill's Weak Rule Utilitarianism

Bentham was John Stuart Mill's tutor and his father James Mill's friend. Mill had an intense childhood, apparently without much emotional warmth. But Bentham's radical liberalism inspired him, and gave him "in a sense, a religion", and he wanted to build upon the insights of the utility principle for social welfare and social reform. Mill campaigned tirelessly amongst other things, for women's rights, the right to contraception and the extension of the democratic vote to all educated people.

Mill is well aware of the defects in Bentham's utilitarianism. Particularly Mill argues:

1. Pleasure and happiness are not the same.

2. Calculating happiness in utils is difficult, so Mill never attempts it.

3. Maximising happiness includes some idea of social utility or general welfare.

4. This general welfare is best served by following rules that experience has proved contribute to happiness.

5. These rules should include those that guarantee justice and rights.

Mill defines utility as 'the permanent interests of man as a progressive being' which begs some questions. What does he mean by 'interests'? How 'permanent' do they have to be? What counts as 'progressive'? He seems to be pointing straightaway at a more complex, sophisticated human being than Bentham's sensualist. But Mill is not consistent either in his treatment of happiness as an idea, or on how to apply the idea of maximising happiness.

Mill appears to start out as an act utilitarian who believes pleasures can be designated as either "higher" or "lower" depending on our nobleness of character. He later argues that **VIRTUE** is a key means to obtaining happiness - the virtue of sacrificing one's own happiness to gain the happiness of others, for example, which can produce a greater sense of contentment. Then in the final section on justice he appears to defend the idea of **RIGHTS** and rules as being principles of utility. He seems to transform himself as he writes into a rule utilitarian[7].

---

7 see J.O. Urmson 1953

THE DEFINITION OF HAPPINESS

Mill disagreed with Bentham that "pushpin is as good as poetry" and spent quite a few pages in the second section of his essay arguing for "higher" and "lower" pleasures. Even here Mill is not entirely consistent, as he flits effortlessly in his essay between references to pleasure and happiness, as if they were identical. They are not: pleasure is commonly thought of as a sensation, whereas happiness is more a long-term state, something closer to contentment.

So Mill begins by saying "pleasure, and freedom from pain, are the only things desirable as ends" but then also says "happiness is...moments of rapture...in an existence of few and transitory pains, many and various pleasures, with a predominance of the active over the passive..not to expect more from life than it is capable of bestowing". Here he moves beyond pleasure as a psychological state, and talks about activity and expectations, both very different things to pleasure as feeling.

Was Mill confused? Martha Nussbaum thinks not: she argues that Mill is influenced by Aristotle's Greek teleological idea of **EUDAIMONIA** (well-being or flourishing), discussed in the opening chapter. And Mill is also influenced by Wordsworth, whose poetry helped him recover from a nervous breakdown in his early 20s. Bringing both ideas together succeeds in giving "richness of life and complexity of activity a place they do not have in Bentham, and giving pleasure and the absence of pain and of depression a role that Aristotle never sufficiently mapped out. The result is the basis, at least, for a conception of happiness that is richer than both of its sources - more capable of doing justice to all the elements that thoughtful people have associated with that elusive idea", (Martha Nussbaum ,Daedulus 2004: 69).

HIGHER AND LOWER PLEASURES

Mill argued that if someone experienced the pleasure of poetry (as he had, reading Wordsworth's Lyrical Ballads) and compared it with the pleasure of computer games (for example), then that person, who alone is competent to judge, would always prefer reading Wordsworth. An educated, intelligent person would never swap places with a fool, argued Mill, so there must be some pleasures that are superior to others.

If happiness is the only thing desired for its own sake, and pigs are generally happy to spend all their time eating and sleeping, then what's to say this shouldn't be the goal of human life? Pig level happiness should not be the goal of human life "precisely because a beast's pleasures do not satisfy a human being's conception of happiness" (II. 4). So Mill claims some kinds of pleasures are intrinsically better than others because they are unique to humans. In particular, the best pleasures are those that employ the "higher faculties" to the greatest degree.

"It is better to be a human being dissatisfied than a pig satisfied; better Socrates dissatisfied than a fool satisfied". J.S.Mill

So Mill distinguishes "high quality" from "low quality" pleasures and pains. Pleasures which Mill regards as superior include those associated with intelligence, education, sensitivity to others, a sense of morality and physical health. Inferior pleasures include those arising from sensual indulgence, laziness, selfishness, stupidity and ignorance. Mill would rather have ten minutes of higher intellectual pleasures than a lifetime eating Mars bars. Where Bentham sees pleasure in **QUANTITATIVE** terms (how much?), Mill sees it in **QUALITATIVE** terms (how good?).

How do we know that higher pleasures are better than lower? Only by experiencing both, argues Mill. "it is an unquestionable fact that those who are equally acquainted with and equally capable of appreciating and enjoying both higher and lower "pleasures" do give a most marked preference to the manner of existence which employs their higher faculties." (II.4)

"A being of higher faculties" argues Mill would not want to ever "sink into what he feels to be a lower grade of existence," meaning one in which he cannot exercise his higher faculties. The person experiencing and valuing the higher pleasures enjoys: "A sense of dignity, which all human beings possess in one form or other, and in some, though by no means in exact, proportion to their higher faculties, and which is so essential a part of the happiness of those in whom it is strong that nothing which conflicts with it could be otherwise than momentarily an object of desire to them. Whoever supposes that this preference takes place at a sacrifice of happiness – that the superior being, in anything like equal circumstances, is not happier than the inferior – confounds the two very different ideas of happiness", (II.5).

So Mill justifies the qualitative nature of his hedonism by appealing to a "sense of dignity" human beings experience in "proportion to their higher faculties". This dignity is "so essential a part of the happiness of those in whom it is strong, that nothing which conflicts with it could be an object of desire to them" (II.5). Here he agrees with Aristotle who sees that pleasures "differ in kind; for those derived from noble sources are different from those derived from base sources, and one cannot get the pleasure of the just man without being just" (NE X.3.5).

One wonders, though, whether an inner city rap artist would agree with this refined view of pleasure, and how this squares with Mill's liberalism which held that people should be allowed to pursue what they wanted, as long as it didn't interfere with others.

MILL AND VIRTUE

My argument here is that Mill's idea of happiness is much closer to Aristotle's **EUDAIMONIA** than Bentham's hedonism. This is because Mill shares with Aristotle a belief that virtue is something desirable for its own sake. After bringing up the objection that utilitarianism denies that people desire virtue, Mill counters that utilitarian moralists would hold "that the mind is...not in a state conformable to Utility...unless it does love virtue...as a thing desirable in itself" (II, 5).

Rather than being something separate from happiness, and as such something desired only instrumentally, as a means to being happy, Mill argues that virtue is part of the goal or telos of happiness. Virtue comes to be desired for its own sake, and in doing so, is "desired as part of happiness" (1979: IV, 6). Mill sees virtue as originally not desired as an end in itself, but becoming part of happiness through the habit of desiring it as a way of becoming happy. Aristotle also argues explicitly that not "by nature...do the virtues arise in us; rather we are adapted by nature to receive them, and are made perfect by habit" (NE II.1.1). Mill and Aristotle are saying the same thing: virtue is central, and achieved by experiencing what builds human happiness.

Just as for Mill virtue can be a thing desirable in itself, and thus good for its own sake, Aristotle states that virtue "will be the state of character which makes a man good and which makes him do his own work well" (II 6.1). Doing his own work well means to Aristotle fulfilling his function well, which is by definition an essential part of eudaimonia (happiness or flourishing), the chief good.

In On Liberty, Mill writes: "He who lets the world . . . choose his plan of life for him has no need of any other faculty than the ape-like one of imitation. He who chooses his plan for himself employs all his faculties.

He must use observation to see, reasoning and judgment to foresee, activity to gather materials for decision, discrimination to decide, and when he has decided, firmness and self-control to hold his deliberate decision." (Mill 1975, 56) As a person develops his powers of wisdom and deliberation and comes to enjoy their exercise, he gains the self-esteem that is the basis of a virtuous and well-lived life. And with the essential prudence (a key Greek virtue) comes self-control (the Greek virtue of temperance).

To Mill, then, happiness includes virtue. It is a richer concept than pleasure. Happiness involves the cultivation of character. The superior being, who can appreciate the higher pleasures, gains dignity, self-respect and depth of character which are necessary for the truly happy life. To Mill, happiness is an evaluative concept (we can have good or bad versions of happiness as JCC Smart suggests) and what makes happiness the best sort must include virtues such as practical wisdom, judgement, sympathy and fortitude as well as an appreciation of the higher intellectual pleasures.

Is Mill just being arrogant and elitist in his division between superior and inferior beings, and higher and lower pleasures? What would the fans of computer games say to this argument? Whatever we think of this question, it is clear that Mill's point, that pleasure is not a simple idea as Bentham implied, is surely correct. The goal of happiness must include a discussion of character, and how character is built. In this sense Mill is surely an Aristotelean.

CONSEQUENTIALISM: THE END JUSTIFIES THE MEANS

Classical utilitarians argue that an act is morally right if it maximises the good (pleasure or happiness, depending) and minimises the pain. For an individual this means making a calculation of likely consequences and choosing the best outcome. For society it means aggregating all members of society and making a policy choice which maximises the happiness of the largest number of people. As Mill put it, defending himself against the charge that utilitarianism was a selfish philosophy, it was concerned "not with the agent's own happiness, but with the greatest happiness altogether" (I.3).

Notice that the past is irrelevant to this calculation. Only present and future happiness matter. So if I have promised to go shopping for my mother today (past) and then it is clear that my students would like me to take them out to coffee (future), then the students claim wins in this calculation, because a past promise counts for nothing.

So utilitarianism reduces rightness or wrongness simply to consequences. Past history or the intrinsic nature of the act have become morally irrelevant. I can make as many promises as I like, and I can tell as many lies as I like (which Kant would argue is intrinsically wrong because it destroys the logic of promise-keeping: for a promise to be a promise it has to be kept!). To a natural law theorist this seems a rather narrow view of goodness. Are there not other goods (like life, education, society, to mention three that Aquinas believed were "primary goods")? Indeed Mill implies in his essay that education is a good, as it helps us distinguish between the higher and lower pleasures!

Also, aggregation, the idea of adding up happiness, is also not as simple as we might think. If we are trying to determine the happiness which results from an action, how far into the future do we go? Do we include future generations, for example in the calculation whether to buy a gass-guzzling sports car to please my wife, when I know the carbon imprint will be much greater than a Daewoo Matiz?

And how do I weigh your claims to happiness against someone else's unhappiness? Bentham's hedonic calculus, as an attempt to measure pleasure in hedons or utils, seems doomed to failure for two reasons: first, because the "hedon" for pleasure is about as meaningful as having "bytes" for love. Such states as happiness and love can't be reducible to a unit, because the value of that unit is so subjective. And second, because my happiness versus your misery doesn't appear to be a very moral calculation. Why should I have a right to inflict any misery on you at all? If I do, shouldn't I just refrain from making that choice?

There is a bigger problem with this sort of consequentialist theory, produced by the age-old philosophical dilemma: does the end ever justify the means? Joseph Fletcher thought so, and wrote in **SITUATION ETHICS** "the end justifies the means, and nothing else", as if we were being stupid if we questioned this idea. Surely to torture a suspect when a bomb is ticking in a bus in Whitehall (the means) is justified if lives are saved (the end)?

Consider the following argument in Arthur Koestler's Darkness at Noon (1940). A former revolutionary in Russia is arrested for doubting the idea that the mass murders of the Stalin era, in which an estimated ten million Russians died, was actually justified: "Acting consequentially in the interests of the coming generations, we have laid such terrible privations on the present one that its present average length of life is shortened by a quarter".

In case we think this argument is irrelevant today, consider the US policy of drone warfare. There have been drone strikes, of unmanned aircraft on civilians in the border region of Pakistan. The US President argues that this increases general happiness by reducing civilian deaths and by killing those people who are plotting the death of innocent people.

However, the opposite effect may well be the true consequence. By killing some innocent people and also targeting those not directly involved in conflict (ie unarmed militant leaders) the policy may well ratchet up anger and grievances which fuel the very radicalism the policy is trying to eliminate. Moreover, it is a policy of the powerful against the powerless. Imagine Al Qaeda could send drones over Washington and take out the American leadership. The result wold be an outcry. It is arguable that the end of eliminating terror leaders never justifies the means by which that end is realised.

THE INTEGRITY PROBLEM

Bernard Williams, the English philosopher who died in 2004, produced two dilemmas which go to the heart of this difficulty that consequentialism can ride roughshod over human rights and create some immoral outcomes.

- **EXAMPLE 1 -** George is a scientist who is out of work. He is offered a job in a laboratory which does research into chemical and biological weapons. George is strongly opposed to the manufacture of chemical and biological weapons. If he does not take the job, his wife and his children will suffer. And if he does not take the job, it will be given to someone else who will pursue the research with fewer inhibitions. Should he take the job?

- **EXAMPLE 2 -** Jim is an explorer who stumbles into a South American village where 20 Indians are about to be shot. The captain says that as a mark of honour to Jim as a guest, he will be invited to shoot one of the Indians, and the other 19 will be set free. If Jim refuses, all 20 Indians will be shot. What should Jim do?

"To these dilemmas, it seems to me that utilitarianism replies, in the first case, that George should accept the job, and in the second that Jim should kill the Indian. Not only does utilitarianism give us these answers, but, if the situations are essentially as described and there are no further special features, it regards them, it seems to me, as obviously right answers." (Smart and Williams, 1994)

"A feature of utilitarianism is that it cuts out a kind of consideration which for some others makes a difference to what they feel about such cases: a consideration involving the idea, as we might first and very simply put it, that each of us is specially responsible for what he does, rather than for what other people do. This is an idea closely connected with the value of integrity." (Smart and Williams, 1994)

Williams is arguing that utilitarianism robs us of something essential to our character: our commitment to certain ideals and values which are quite independent of consequences, values such as truth-telling and the sacredness of human life. If you ask me to act outside of my character then you are asking me to do something impossible: to be someone else.

RULE UTILITARIANISM AS AN ANSWER TO THE PROBLEM OF INJUSTICE

To try to eliminate some of the perceived weaknesses of act utilitarianism, Mill proposes a **RULE UTILITARIANISM** which argues that happiness is best maximised by mostly following certain rules, such as the rules "do not lie" and "keep your promises". Rule utilitarianism holds that an act is right if it conforms with a set of rules the adoption of which produces the happiest outcome. In order to strengthen this argument, Mil also employs the idea of **VIRTUE**.

Mill takes trouble to argue in the last section of his essay Utilitarianism that unhappiness is caused by selfishness, by people "acting only for themselves", and that for a person to be happy they need "to cultivate a fellow feeling with the collective interests of mankind" and "in the golden rule of Jesus we find the whole ethics of utility". We might add that the Situation Ethicist Joseph Fletcher claims Jesus as his own, as does Immanuel Kant who argued that Matthew 7:23 "do to others as you would have them do to you" was very close to his first formulation of the categorical imperative, that of universalisability.

Perhaps Mill recognised that utilitarian philosophy contradicted the argument in his, in my view, much greater essay On Liberty, where he argues that the only justification for infringing personal liberty is to prevent harm to others. So the utilitarian argument for locking up thousands of Japanese Americans during the second world war, that some of them might be spies, would have no justification according to Mill's On Liberty.

In Utilitarianism Mill defends the concept of rights in terms of utility: "To have a right, then, is, I conceive, to have something which society should defend me in possession of. If the objector asks why? I can give no other answer than general utility", (V).

So Mill appears to be arguing here that general happiness requires that some rights be guaranteed, such as the rights to life, liberty, and property. So the rules become: life is sacred and can never be taken away, freedom is a right which can only be infringed under particular circumstances, and property is defended by rules of access and entitlement.

Yet a little later in the essay, Mill appears to argue that these rights can be infringed for the greater good.

"Justice is a name for certain moral requirements, which, regarded collectively, stand higher in the scale of social utility, and are therefore of more paramount obligation, than any others: though particular cases may occur in which some other social duty is so important as to overrule any one of the general maxims of justice. Thus to save a life it may not only be allowable, but a duty, to steal, or take by force, the necessary food or medicine, or to kidnap, or compel to officiate, the only qualified medical practitioner", (V).

Mill goes on to stress the importance of rules underpinning the idea of justice, which he has attempted to show are grounded on the greatest happiness principle. These rules, he says, have a "more absolute obligation", implying that in cases of conflicting claims to right action (such as occurred for Jim with the indians) the rules of justice and implicit rights to life, liberty and property must take precedence.

"I account the justice which is grounded on utility to be the chief

part, and incomparably the most sacred and binding part, of all morality. Justice is a name for certain classes of moral rules, which concern the essentials of human well-being more nearly, and are therefore of more absolute obligation, than any other rules for the guidance of life. " (V)

The objection here is that in arguing for rules Mill applies deontological (duty-based) principles for justification – so the 'not stealing' rule is justified not because we know that this will maximise utility (which we can't know without evidence) but because it is not rational to have a society in which everyone steals. Mill counters this objection with a strong social utility argument: only such rules make for a happy (secure, confident, stable) society.

MULTILEVEL UTILITARIANISM

Mill likens the rules we need to follow to a ship's almanac which guides the ship as to tide times and heights. We use generations of past experience to form rules, so we don't have to do a calculation to know whether murder or theft is "right". We inherit beliefs "and the beliefs which have thus come down are the rules of morality for the multitude" (JS Mill). These are not fixed but "admit of continual improvement" – so they are not absolute, just as the tidal almanac is always being revised so isn't fixed.

"Nobody argues that the art of navigation is not founded on astronomy, because sailors cannot wait to calculate the Nautical Almanack. Being rational creatures, they go to sea with it ready calculated; and all rational creatures go out upon the sea of life with their minds made up on the common questions of right and wrong. Whatever we adopt as the fundamental principle of morality, we require subordinate principles to apply it by; the impossibility of doing without them, being common to all systems, can afford no argument against any one in particular; but gravely to argue as if no such secondary principles could be had, and as if mankind had remained till now, and always must remain, without drawing any general conclusions from the experience of human life, is as high a pitch, I think, as absurdity has ever reached in philosophical controversy". (II).

The **FUNDAMENTAL PRINCIPLE** is utility (or the Greatest Happiness Principle) and then **SECONDARY PRINCIPLES** (rules) come from this and are constantly evaluated against the first principle. Just as navigation is based on astronomy doesn't mean the sailor goes back to the stars every time – no he uses an almanac – so, argues Mill, human beings follow a code book of rules passed down from previous generations as the best way to be happy. But the presence of the Almanac doesn't stop a sailor using his or her judgement - and looking at circumstances.

So Mill's can be described as a multilevel approach. This multilevel approach can be summed up thus (and so is referred to as weak rule utilitarianism, as the rules are not absolute):

- **LEVEL 1** - follow general rules that past experience has shown to promote happiness.

- **LEVEL 2** - when faced with a moral dilemma or a strong case for breaking these rules, revert to act utilitarianism. Reason on a case by case basis according to the one good of maximising happiness or welfare.

Mill believes we should follow these general rules or secondary principles automatically most of the time. Then we should periodically step back and review whether the principle continues to satisfy the greatest happiness principle. We also set aside these rules or secondary principles and make direct appeal to the principle of utility in unusual cases, when it is clear that the effects of sticking to the principle would be disastrous and in cases in which secondary principles, each of which has a utilitarian justification, conflict (ii 19, 24-25). The rest of the time we should regulate our conduct according to these secondary principles without referring to the utilitarian first principle.

David Brink concludes "regulating one's behaviour in this way by secondary principles is what will best promote happiness". David Brink agrees with J.O. Urmson[8] that Mill should be classified as a weak rule utilitarian, a view confirmed in Mill's Essay on Bentham:

"We think utility, or happiness, much too complex and indefinite an end to be sought except through the medium of various secondary ends. Those who adopt utility as a standard can seldom apply it truly except through the secondary principles; those who reject it, generally do no more than erect those secondary principles into first principles. It is when two or more of the secondary principles conflict, that a direct appeal to some first principle becomes necessary; and then commences the practical importance of the utilitarian controversy".

It seems clear that Mill is assigning a key role to secondary principles or rules in a utilitarian calculation. The rules are weak because they can be broken when the situation demands it - and on these occasions Mill wants us to go back to being **ACT UTILITARIANS**.

---

8 *The influential article by J.O.Urmson,* The Interpretation of the Philosophy of J.S. Mill (1953)

DUTY VERSUS PLEASURE

W.D. Ross (1877-1971) argued for a **DEONTOLOGICAL** (duty-based) form of intuitionism. An **INTUITION** is an in-built perception of right and wrong. We know in a general sense what our **PRIMA FACIE** duties (Latin for "at first sight") are, and then we know by intuition how to rank them in importance - to know which one to apply to which situation. Ross' theory allows us a way out when two rules conflict (do I lie to save a friend?). By ranking duties we can argue that one duty is more important than another (saving a life is more important than not lying).

In daily life we often feel the clash between duty and pleasure. In the morning I would prefer to lie in bed than walk the dog on a cold day; in the evening you would rather watch Hollyoaks than finish your ethics essay. Mill suggested in the quote above that we sometimes have a duty to steal in order to save a life, perhaps hinting that there is some kind of moral hierarchy. At the top, we place preservation of life, and lower down, the rule "thou shalt not steal".

W.D. Ross suggests we have prima facie (arising at first sight) duties. I may have a prima facie duty to keep my promise to meet you for coffee today, but if my child is injured in a car accident my duty is to be by his side, even if this means missing my coffee appointment. I may have promised to meet you, but I can break that promise if a more pressing obligation appears, such as helping my child recover. In cases of conflict, I make a decision based on intuition to ignore my prima facie duty. My duty to help my child (one prima facie duty) overrides my duty to keep my promise (another prima facie duty) in the above example.

Ross argues that utilitarianism "seems to simplify unduly our relations to our fellows".

"It says, in effect, that the only significant relation in which my neighbours stand to me is that of being possible beneficiaries by my action. They do stand in this relation to me, and this relation is morally significant. But they may also stand to me in the relation of promisee to promiser, or creditor to debtor, of wife to husband, of child to parent, of friend to friend, of fellow-countryman to fellow-countryman, and the like; and each of these relations is the foundation of a prima-facie duty",
W.D.Ross (1930:25).

Putting these two features together, we can say that utilitarianism is unable to explain what promising is. A promise is a way of creating a commitment, of putting yourself under an obligation to someone.

Similarly a utilitarian cannot explain what faithfulness is, what a debt is, what gratitude is, what desert is.

Ross gives a list of things he considers prima facie obligations: keeping a promise, returning a favour, promoting the good of others. These obligations are intuitively certain and are of a general sort, and according to Ross, we remain certain that they are obligations even when, in extreme circumstances such as I mentioned above, we are compelled to break them.

"The moral order expressed in these propositions is just as much part of the fundamental nature of the universe...as the spatial structure expressed in geometry", (W.D.Ross, 1930:29).

Ross therefore gives us a way out of moral dilemmas, and we might call this another multilevel approach. Level 1 is "follow the prima facie duty" and level 2 is "make a judgment when two duties conflict". His is a deontological approach, but if you followed the above argument, Ross is not an absolutist, as you can break a promise in some circumstances.

Ross was also an intuitionist who argued for moral feelings which were innate to all of us. This brief discussion of his views reminds us again that there are three basic ways of establishing the "good": by **CONSEQUENCES**, as in utilitarian consequentialism, **RULES** as in Kantian deontology, and **FEELINGS** or intuitions, as in Ross' deontology.

STRENGTHS AND WEAKNESSES

Strengths

- **SIMPLICITY** - it gives a clear basis for making policy decisions and is still instrumental in framing laws on ethical issues, such as the Abortion Act 1967 and the Human Fertilisation and Embryology Act 2008.

- **EQUALITY** - "everyone to count as one, and no-one as more than one" (Bentham). The happiness of the individual is of equal weight irrespective of wealth, status or education. And your view of pleasure is as good as mine - it's your desires that count.

- **BENEVOLENCE** - it seeks to promote concern for the happiness of others and the happiness of society generally, which as Mill pointed out, is a selfless moral stance. Mill argues that utilitarianism is based on a "general sympathy" we have for one another (sympathy is, of course, a moral virtue).

Weaknesses

- **LACK OF INTEGRITY** - it suffers, as Bernard Williams points out, from being an instrumental, means to an end philosophy, which fails to take into account moral character and the importance of integrity (being true to one's own beliefs).

- **INJUSTICE** - it suffers from the possibility of immoral outcomes, where a person or groups of people(Jews or negroes) become scapegoats for the happiness of the majority. So moral fanatics such as Stalin or Hitler or the lynch mob in the southern states could claim they were acting to maximize happiness.

- **CALCULATION PROBLEMS** - utilitarianism requires constant calculations, but whom do we include, and how do we know exactly what the outcomes of our action will be?

Lawrence Hinman of the University of San Diego concludes that: "Utilitarianism is most appropriate for policy decisions, as long as a strong notion of fundamental human rights guarantees that it will not violate the rights of small minorities".

Maybe it was this sort of conclusion which Mill was groping towards when he wrote his seemingly contradictory essays On Liberty and Utilitarianism.

SUMMARY

BENTHAM (1748-1832)	MILL (1806-1873)
• Empirical (measure goodness a posteriori)	• Empirical (against the intuitionists)
• Hedonistic (pleasure based)	• Eudaimonistic (happiness based)
• Consequentialist	• Consequentialist
• Act utilitarian	• Rule utilitarian

Intrinsic good – pleasure	Intrinsic good – happiness
Two sovereign masters – pain and pleasure. One intrinsic good – happiness.	Happiness is more than just pleasure, but about having goals and virtues as well as pleasure.
NB Psychological hedonism	NB Aristotlean eudaimonism

Act utilitarian	Rule utilitarian
Happiness is maximised by actions that produce the maximum amount of pleasure, and minimum pain, for the greatest number of people.	Happiness is maximised by following social rules, beliefs and practices which past experience have shown create happiness.

BENTHAM (1748-1832)	MILL (1806-1873)
Quantitative pleasure	**Qualitative pleasure**
Pleasure could be calculated by the **Hedonic calculus** (acronym P.R.R.I.C.E.D.)	Pleasure needs to be defined carefully to avoid creating a "swinish philosophy" – so Mill distinguishes between higher pleasures (music, art, poetry) and lower pleasures (food, drink, sex). Higher pleasures are more valuable.
Goodness as pleasure	**Goodness as happiness**
What makes an action good is the balance of pleasure over pain for the maximum number of people. Bentham is a psychological hedonist – pleasure is our motivation (not duty, God, or loyalties).	What makes an action good is the balance of happiness over unhappiness which it produces, where happiness is close to Aristotle's idea of eudaimonia (includes goals, expectations, and character).
Justice ignored	**Justice addressed**
Bentham doesn't address the issue of the rights of the minority which may be infringed by maximising pleasure of the majority (eg lynchings).	Mill was concerned about rights and justice and argued that happiness could only be maximised by having certain rights guaranteed and laws or rules which promoted general happiness.

BENTHAM (1748-1832)	MILL (1806-1873)
Motivation – self-interest	**Motivation – sympathy**
Bentham saw utility in narrow, individualistic terms and would agree with Margaret Thatcher's saying– "there is no thing as society, just individuals". He was suspicious of sympathy/antipathy as internal guides to action as they often conflicted with the external test of utility.	Mill argued that we have a general sympathy for other human beings which gave us the motivation to seek the general good, not just our own.
Single level - Act Utilitarianism	**Multilevel – weak Rule Utilitarianism**
Bentham's theory operates only on the level of individual choice and pleasure applied to action. Such action can be influenced by laws and taboos – but remains an individual choice.	Level 1: The follow rules experience have been shown to create happiness
	Level 2: where a strong utilitarian reason exists, break the rule in this circumstance.

BENTHAM (1748-1832)	MILL (1806-1873)
Criticisms of Bentham	**Criticisms of Mill**
Assumes pleasure is the only good (what of duty, sacrifice etc?).	Assumes happiness is the only good (what of virtue?).
Assumes pleasure and happiness are identical (they're not – think of an athlete in training).	Assumes higher pleasures are more desired than lower pleasures.
Believes we can calculate pleasure empirically (maybe we can't).	Makes the difficulty of calculation even more problematic by this higher/lower distinction.
Ignores problems of injustices which utilitarianism produces (see Bernard Williams' critique).	Rule utilitarianism collapses into act utilitarianism when we face moral dilemmas.

SELF-TEST: KEY TERMS

consequentialism - empirical - act utilitarianism - rule utilitarianism - hedonism - felicific calculus - eudaimonia - higher pleasures - lower pleasures

SELF-TEST QUESTIONS

1. What is the difference between pleasure and happiness?

2. Is it possible to measure pleasure?

3. Explain how act utilitarianism differs from rule utilitarianism.

4. Explain Mill's view that there are higher and lower pleasures.

5. Why is justice so important to Mill?

6. "Equality is the basis for utilitarian ethics". Explain why.

7. Does the end justify the means? Apply this idea to a modern situation.

8. Why would a utilitarian ever save a stranger?

9. Utilitarian ethics is empirical and naturalistic. What do these words mean?

10. Do the strengths of utilitarian ethics outweigh the weaknesses?

KEY QUOTES

1. *"For the dictates of utility are neither more nor less than the dictates of the most extensive and enlightened (that is well-advised) benevolence."* Jeremy Bentham

2. *"Utilitarian moralists have gone beyond almost all others in affirming that the motive has nothing to do with the morality of the action, though much with the worth of the agent."* J.S.Mill

3. *"I find it hard to believe that an action or rule can be right or wrong if there is no good or evil connected with it".* William Frankena

4. *"Take any demand, however slight, which any creature, however weak, may make. Ought it not, for its own sake, to be satisfied? If not, prove why not".* William James

5. *"Bentham's philosophy may be too simplistic and too complicated. It may be too simplistic in that there are values other than pleasure, and it seems too complicated in its artificial hedonic calculus".* Louis Pojman

6. *"Utilitarianism has two virtues...it gives us a clear decision procedure in arriving at our answer about what to do. The second virtue appeals to our sense that morality is made for*

humans (and other animals?) and that morality is not so much about rules as about helping people and alleviating the suffering of the world". Louis Pojman

7. *"In the long run, and when reinterpreted by socialists like Robert Owen, utilitarianism in practice did some good, even though it never made much sense as a philosophy. In the short term, it was just one more disaster inflicted upon the British working class." George Lichtheimm*

8. *"I do not care about the greatest good for the greatest number . . . Most people are poop-heads: I do not care about them at all." James Alan Gardener - Ascending.*

9. *"If we British were Utilitarians we would have to believe that imprisoning the innocent and torturing suspects was justified if the Home Secretary thought it a good thing for our peace of mind." William Donaldson*

10. *"The end may justify the means as long as there is something that justifies the end." Leon Trotsky*

Preference Utilitarianism

We have seen that utilitarian ethics applies an **EMPIRICAL** measure to gain some idea of objective goodness or social welfare. Where Bentham takes the balance of pleasure over pain, Peter Singer bases his ethic on one good of maximising the first preferences of sentient beings. "It is preference utilitarianism that we reach by universalising our own interests - if that is, we take the plausible move of taking a person's interest to be what, on balance, and after reflection on all the relevant facts, a person prefers", (Practical Ethics, PE 94).

He claims the following features for his theory:

1. **OBJECTIVE** - as there is one impersonal standard of evaluation.

2. **EMPIRICAL** - as the means of calculation is to add up preferences. Singer argues this is much easier to apply than Bentham's measure of psychological states of pleasure.

3. **EGALITARIAN** - as the interests of the poor are equally as important as the rich and animals are as morally significant as humans.

4. **CONSEQUENTIALIST** - as it is the consequences of decisions which render them desirable or undesirable.

However, who is included in the idea of personhood crucially affects the morality of an action. Who has moral relevance depends crucially on the ability to state a preference and "have an **INTEREST**". Rather than base his utilitarian ethics on an idea of happiness or pleasure, which are hard to define and measure, Singer bases his ethics on a conscious state of choosing as "beings who cannot see themselves as entities with a future cannot have any preferences about their own future existence".

As we shall see, this includes, foetuses, children up to four weeks of age, those who have lost hope, and those with Alzheimer's disease or in a persistent vegetative state. In this chapter I will argue that personhood is as hard to define and problematic as happiness, and that Singer's treatment of personhood is inconsistent. He is in fact creating a two-tier concept of humanity which gives absolute authority to those defined into the higher tier.

THE PRINCIPLE OF EQUAL CONSIDERATION OF INTERESTS AND THE UNIVERSAL PERSPECTIVE

Singer does not treat **OBJECTIVITY** in the same way as a natural law theorist who sees an objective law in the way the universe is set up. In contrast with the utilitarian Bentham, he claims a way of establishing objectivity in ethics by appealing to interests. And although the perception of an interest may appear to be subjective, Singer stresses that objectivity in ethics requires a universal viewpoint - "the point of view of the universe" as he calls it.

"I have been arguing against the view that value depends entirely on my own subjective desires. Yet I am not defending the objectivity of ethics in the traditional sense. Ethical truths are not written into the fabric of the universe: to that extent the subjectivist is correct. If there were no beings with desires or preferences of any kind, nothing would be of value and ethics would lack all content" (PE 267).

The ability to see others' interests as significant leads to the conclusion that my perspective, choices and interest have no greater validity than anyone else's. Bentham's "everyone to count as one" becomes "everyone's interests are to be counted equally".

Singer continues:

> *'Reason makes it possible for us to see ourselves in this way because, by thinking about my place in the world, I am able to see that I am just one being among others, with interests and desires like others. I have a personal perspective on the world, from which my interests are at the front and centre of the stage, the interests of my family and friends are close behind, and the interests of strangers are pushed to the back and sides'.*

> *'But reason enables me to see that others have similarly subjective perspectives, and that from 'the point of view of the universe' my perspective is no more privileged than theirs. Thus my ability to reason shows me the possibility of detaching myself from my own perspective and shows me what the universe might look like if I had no personal perspective' (PE page 267).*

On the other hand, once there are beings with desires, there are values that are not only the subjective values of each individual being. Singer argues that the possibility of being led, by reasoning, to the point of view of the universe provides as much "objectivity" as there can be. This gives us a cause as well as a basis for reasoning. Our cause is the "reduction of pain and suffering wherever it is to be found".

"When my ability to reason shows me that the suffering of another being is very similar to my own suffering and (in an appropriate case) matters just as much to that other being as my own suffering matters to me, then my reason is showing me something that is undeniably true. I can still choose to ignore it, but then I can no longer deny that my perspective is a narrower and more limited one than it could be. This may not be enough to yield an objectively true ethical position. (One can ask: what is so good about having a broader and more all-encompassing perspective?) But it is as close to an objective basis for ethics as there is to find", (The Good Life).

So everyone's interests are to count equally - as long as we can express those interests and state preferences. For an action to be moral, "I must choose the course of action that has the best consequences, on balance, for all those affected" (PE page 13), where best consequences equate to fulfilling interests and preferences. The idea of interest is agent-neutral: "An interest is an interest whoever's interest it may be" (PE page 21).

This is not the same as strict equality. Imagine two people lying injured on the ground, the first thing a triage nurse will do is assess the severity of the wounds. Those who are most severely wounded get preferential treatment, double doses of morphine. Both patients have equal rights to treatment, but the second needs the treatment more urgently.

Therefore it is the consideration of interests that is equal, not the people themselves. This leads to the conclusion that those who can no longer express interests, articulate them and indicate unambiguously what they are lose all intrinsic moral value. Also, controversially, babies up to four weeks old have no right to life. The decision to kill lies with the parents and if any wrong is done to them, it is done to the parents rather than the child as it is the parents' own **PREFERENCES** about whether a child should live or die which determines the morality of infanticide.

THE IDEA OF PERSONHOOD

Singer argues for two levels of personhood which create two levels of decision-making. A level 1 'person' (my term) is defined as "a being with certain characteristics such as rationality and self-awareness". (Rethinking Life and Death, page 180).

Such people have preferences which they can state and should be honoured by everyone else - hence level 1 people produce the idea of "preference utilitarianism". Elsewhere he speaks of a "sense of biography", of "past and future", or "entities with a future" (PE page 94). Even a new-born baby is denied the full right to life in that it cannot be considered a person as it is, according to Singer, not self-aware. In this case the self-aware parent can make a preference to have a child killed (infanticide for the disabled for example). On this Kevin Toolis has written:

"Parents would be free to kill their infants if they did not like their skin, hair colour, sex or the length of their legs. His philosophy justifies the infanticide practised in China against baby girls during the years of the One Child policy." (The Guardian, Nov 6, 1999).

If a foetus, a new born infant, a severely disabled person cannot state

69

preferences, they are not "persons". They have moral value only in so far as someone else prefers them to live (parents, friends, family). We can call these (my term) level 2 beings.

Notice that Singer seems to be inconsistent here. He both argues for a process of growing into personhood, and also for an arbitrary point where rights are given at "about four weeks". He argues in the context of abortion (as does Jonathan Glover in Causing Death and Saving Lives) that we should think of personhood as a process, so that the foetus at 18 weeks has greater moral worth than the collection of embryonic cells at 14 days. The new born infant has more worth than the foetus. And at "about four weeks" full sanctity of personhood kicks in. The give away word "about" betrays the looseness of his thinking. Why not four and half, or five, or nine weeks?

Also, Singer seems to attribute self-awareness to the great apes. But if they are self-aware and rational it's clear they are not as self-aware and rational as humans. Let's say they are 30% as self-aware. Why attribute absolute value to them, and not to the disabled infant who may be 50% as aware as the able-bodied one? And what about the normal infant of three weeks who in terms of that stage of development is 100% self-aware, rational and sentient? Why give the newborn full personhood rights at four weeks, even though the interests they express are only done so in a way difficult to determine (a cry, a shriek)? Surely, even if we agree with Singer's logic, we should be flexible about when personhood status is given to infants - depending on the stages of child development?

THE REPLACEABILITY PRINCIPLE FOR LEVEL 2 BEINGS

If you do not conform to the level 1 definition of a person above, implied by Singer's quote above as "entities with a future", and so are (by his definition) a sub-person due to disability, lack of self-awareness, then the balance of pleasure and pain applies. If you, as an infant, are killed and replaced by a happier infant (for example, disabled replaced by able-bodied child) then this is a moral good, according to Singer. We could call this the **REPLACEABILITY ARGUMENT** (and it applies to the chicken as well - kill a chicken and replace it with a happy chicken. Of course, Singer values animal rights so you must kill the chicken painlessly).

This is a version of Bentham's hedonic act utilitarian ethic. Note how, as with Bentham, the **PROBLEM OF CALCULATION** resurfaces here as soon as we try to forecast future pleasure and happiness of two people (I suppose we should call the disabled person an "entity" and the three week old infant an "almost person").

So Singer has been referred to as a consequential-utilitarian ethicist. This is only partially correct. Singer is a preference utilitarian for level 1 beings and a hedonic consequentialist for lower order beings. The preference utilitarian considers consequences only in so far as a choice affects other people in a way they would never like or choose. There are however serious calculation problems for preference and hedonic utilitarianism (we cannot know the future and are making a best guess), and serious objections can be made to the concept of personhood which is so fundamental to the multilevel approach of Peter Singer.

It's also not clear, for example, what happens if the government thinks my own preference (for smoking dope or driving my car too fast at night) is undesirable because of its effects on society generally. Are my preferences limited by law? What if the law is unjust or the government's calculation immoral (eg preferences for lynching people were tolerated in the American deep south for many years)?

As, by definition, there can be no intrinsic good in preference utilitarianism (pleasure/pain is irrelevant now), it seems that the choice could be for anything - just as long as it's a private choice and doesn't affect the choices of others in the future.

ANIMALS AS PERSONS

Singer's definition of personhood as "entities with a future" allows him to conclude that "some non-human animals are persons". He discusses a number of laboratory experiments involving chimpanzees which indicates an ability to use language to communicate. It is not only in laboratories that Singer deduces personhood characteristics, but also in the co-operative behaviour and deceptive behaviour of chimps in the wild, which "points to the conclusion that they possess both memory of the past and expectations of the future, and that they are self-aware, that they form intentions and act on them" (PE page 115).

The doctrine of the sanctity of life needs rephrasing, Singer argues, as the "doctrine of the sanctity of personal life" (PE page 117). It is only those beings with characteristics of personhood that should be protected. "Some members of other species are persons, some members of our own species are not" (PE, 117). So it follows that killing a chimp is worse morally than killing a severely disabled child. It is possible (though Singer describes it as "speculative") to extend this self-conscious personhood to dogs, cats, and pigs. For this reason Singer argues in The Great Ape project :

"We demand the extension of the community of equals to include all great apes: human beings, chimpanzees, gorillas and orang-utans. "The community of equals" is the moral community within which we accept certain basic principles or rights as governing our relations with each other and enforceable at law. Among these principles or rights are the following:

1. The Right to Life

2. The Protection of Individual Liberty

3. The Prohibition of Torture

At present, only members of the species Homo Sapiens are regarded as members of the community of equals. The inclusion, for the first time, of nonhuman animals into this community is an ambitious project. The chimpanzee, the gorilla, and the orang-utan, Pongo pygmaeus, are the closest relatives of our species."[9]

Let's examine the logic of the argument here.

1. A person is someone with a sense of past and future, who forms intentions and is self-aware.

2. Some animals possess the characteristics of persons.

9 P. Cavalieri, P. Singer (Ed.), The Great Ape Project. Equality Beyond Humanity, New York: St Martin'S

3. Only persons have absolute sanctity of life.

4. Therefore, we should not kill some animals.

The second premise is the most controversial. Despite the evidence offered by Singer, how do we know animals are self-aware rather than reactive? Are their "intentions" those that can be articulated with reasons? Even a chimp would be hard-pressed to answer the question: "why did you do that?"

Moreover, premise 2 seems rather arbitrary. In calling animals persons we seem to be giving them human status, implying they are like us in every relevant way. Surely the most important way is to **UNIVERSALISE** behaviour as an ethical judgement - which implies that these animals would never kill members of their own species (or even related species). Although it may appear speciest (prejudiced against a member of another species), there is a moral difference between a human being and an ape. The difference is one of genes and biology. It is to do with the rational ability to universalise actions - the basis of moral thinking. Their inability to think morally is arguably the key reason why apes can never be counted as persons.

In the requirement of consistency, if utilitarians are to oppose the killing of animals, then they should also oppose the killing of animals by other animals. Animals are either persons or they are not - this is Singer's very point. Chimps (who are persons) are notoriously aggressive towards monkeys, for example, and kill and eat them. If Singer is to be consistent, he should try these chimps for murder for breaking the sanctity of life of another higher order primate. One wonders how the chimp will plead.

SINGER'S FOUR PRINCIPLES

Singer has identified four principles to guide our choice or preference when we are acting as act utilitarians and making choices on behalf of those (humans or animals) who cannot state preferences themselves.

1. "Pain is bad, and similar amounts of pain are equally bad, no matter whose pain it might be... Conversely pleasure and happiness are good, no matter whose pleasure or happiness they might be".

2. "Humans are not the only beings capable of feeling pain or of suffering".

3. "When we consider how serious it is to take a life, we should look not at the race, sex, species to which that being belongs but at the characteristics of the individual being killed".

4. "We are responsible not only for what we do, but also for what we could have prevented."

There are two major problems with the first principle. How do we quantify "similar amounts" of pain or pleasure? When non-persons cannot express themselves and articulate the level of pain, we have to make our own judgement. Secondly how do we compare people, or animals when a given act involves pleasure to some and pain to others? Very few acts involve an unambiguous increase in pleasure and/or reduction in pain. To calculate the Benthamite "greatest happiness of the greatest number" in these circumstances will be almost impossible . To apply this principle in particular circumstances means an arbitrary value of hedons has to be imputed to the pain and pleasure of the individuals involved in the given action.

The second principle is the one on which there is the greatest degree of agreement. Singer asserts that "all the mammals and birds that we habitually eat" can feel pain. Some biologists have argued that animals without well developed nervous systems (like insects) do not feel pain. However Singer defines pain to include suffering and distress of all kinds, so it should be applied to every sentient being even if we are not sure if they enjoy pleasure or suffer pain.

The third principle amplifies the ethic attached to killing, which is the one ethic on which all ethical systems take a stand. The Bible verse "thou shalt not murder" applies only to human beings, and that too with some exceptions (as in the conduct of war, or the punishment of criminals, or with respect to slaves). Singer's important change is to extend non-killing to animals.

But Singer does not have a blanket opposition to all killing (for example, you can kill a chicken painlessly and replace it with another happy chicken). Nor does he oppose animal experiments as long as net welfare is increased by them. The absolute prohibition only applies to higher order primates.

The fourth principle involves acts and omissions. We are responsible for what we do but also for the choices we fail to make. He gives the example of a person who does not save a drowning child if he could have saved this child without danger to himself as morally guilty.

Singer's drowning example can lead to some complications. Suppose that the spectator is confronted with a drowning dog and a drowning small child. He can save one but not both. How would Singer's ethics resolve which of these two the spectator should save? According to Singer, both have identifiable future interests.

PREFERENCES OR INTERESTS?

Is a preference the same as an **INTEREST**? Interest is an ambiguous idea with three meanings, and it would appear that a "preference" only makes sense in terms of the third meaning.

1. The interest which stems from mere existence, for example, the interest of an ash tree to live. We can call this **BIOLOGICAL** interest.

2. Interests of sentient beings who can suffer the evil of pain and the good of pleasure. Singer calls this "having an interest". For example, Singer argues "A stone does not have interests because it cannot suffer. Nothing that we can do to it could possibly affect its welfare. The capacity for suffering and enjoyment is, however, not only necessary, but also sufficient for us to say that a being has interests—at an absolute minimum, an interest in not suffering". (PE, 8) Let's call this **SENTIENT** interest.

3. Taking and creating an interest through choice and thought. We can call this **RATIONAL** interest. I take an interest in my health, clothes, education. You have corresponding obligations to allow my freedom subject to some limitations (such as not causing pain to others). Here Singer equates rational interest with desire. "If we define ''interests'' broadly enough, so that we count anything people desire as in their interests ... then it would seem that at this pre-ethical stage, only one's interests can be relevant to the decision".

Now, a **PREFERENCE** only relates to the third type of interest - an entity which takes or expresses a choice expresses an interest in something. So animals may have an interest in survival but they cannot express an interest as a choice or articulate it as a justification for their behaviour.

What has happend here is that Singer seems to have confused two meanings of interest. Is it morally significant that animals feel pain even though they cannot state preferences? Is an animal's experience of pain equivalent to human experiences of pain? This is hard to prove, and seems to suggest a speculative basis for Singer's view of moral worth.

Moreover, we as humans are imputing interests to animals and trees - as they cannot articulate them themselves. This suggests a fallacy of **ANTHROPOMORPHISM** - of attributing human qualities to non-human things.

WORLD POVERTY

Peter Singer advocates a radical redistribution of wealth and income, and if necessary of migrant populations. "The principle of equal consideration of interests points to a world in which all countries continue to accept refugees until they are reduced to the same standard of poverty and overcrowding as the third world countries from which the refugees are seeking to flee".[10]

Singer concludes that this may sound unrealistic, but it is nonetheless rational.

> *"Now, evolutionary psychologists tell us that human nature just isn't sufficiently altruistic to make it plausible that many people will sacrifice so much for strangers. On the facts of human nature, they might be right, but they would be wrong to draw a moral conclusion from those facts. If it is the case that we ought to do things that, predictably, most of us won't do, then let's face that fact head-on. Then, if we value the life of a child more than going to fancy restaurants, the next time we dine out we will know that we could have done something better with our money. If that makes living a morally decent life extremely arduous, well, then that is the way things are. If we don't do it, then we should at least know that we are failing to live a morally decent life —not because it is good to wallow in guilt but because knowing where we should be going is the first step toward heading in that direction".*

---

10 P. Singer, *Practical Ethics,*p. 261

STRENGTHS

- **EQUALITY** - Singer's equal consideration of interests provides an impartial "base position" for arriving at moral decisions, which avoids issues of partiality, speciesm and power.

- **CONSISTENCY** - Singer's preference utilitarianism gives us a consistent method for judging ethical dilemmas, such as whether a disabled child should be allowed to live or whether euthanasia should be seen as acceptable.

- **RADICALISM** - Singer, in the tradition of Bentham and Mill, offers a radical solution to world poverty, animal welfare, and issues of human sexuality. He even suggests bestiality is morally acceptable as long as no harm is done to the animal. In an age when few ethicists seem able to produce radical solutions to the world's problems, Singer has the courage to go where others fear to tread.

WEAKNESSES

- **DEVALUING HUMAN LIFE** - the "commodification" of human life denies the inherent dignity that all humans, even foetuses or comatose patients, possess equally. Singer appears to make big assumptions, for example, about the nature of disabled people, their conscious life, and the idea of a life worth living.

- **INCONSISTENCIES** - Singer awards personhood status to human babies at four weeks. But it seems inconsistent to award small infants lesser status and animals (monkeys, apes for example) higher status. It may even be a form of speciesm he himself condemns - the tyranny of the self-conscious, future-aware form of human being, a higher form of being who has absolute rights to make choices on behalf of others (foetuses, severely disabled, alzheimer victims, and animals who aren't persons).

- **PARTIALITY** - intuitively we treat our own relatives differently, contrary to Singer's equality principle. In other words, we are partial in our moral choices towards those nearest to us. Singer admits to doing the same when his mother contracted Alzheimer's. His ethically objective position suggests she should be replaced by a happier human being, or the resources used in her care relocated to aid higher-order beings. Singer couldn't bring himself to advocate euthanasia for his own mother.

SELF-TEST: KEY TERMS

interests - preferences - universal viewpoint - persons - entities - replaceability argument - sentience

SELF-TEST QUESTIONS

1. What does it mean to maximise preferences?

2. "Preference utilitarianism is consequentialist". Explain

3. Explain the "universal viewpoint".

4. How does Singer define persons?

5. Why according to Singer should some animals be classified as "persons"?

6. How does Singer justify abortion?

7. How does preference utilitarianism differ from Mill's rule utilitarianism?

8. Singer gives a third of his income away to the poor. Should we do the same?

9. "Killing severely disabled infants is morally acceptable". Evaluate this view.

10. "Quality of life is more important than sanctity of life". Is it?

KEY QUOTES

1. *"An ethical judgment that is no good in practice must suffer from a theoretical defect". Peter Singer*

2. *"Killing a newborn baby is never equivalent to killing a person, that is, a being who wants to go on living." Peter Singer*

3. *"I feel the duty to reaffirm strongly that the intrinsic value and personal dignity of every human being do not change, no matter what the concrete circumstances of his or her life. A man, even if seriously ill or disabled in the exercise of his highest functions, is and always will be a man, and he will never become a "vegetable" or an "animal." Even our brothers and sisters who find themselves in the clinical condition of a "vegetative state" retain their human dignity in all its fullness". Pope John Paul II*

4. *"It appears that utilitarianism replaces the value of partial relationships with a cold, moral bureaucracy, in which everyone is treated equally. This flaw in utilitarianism serves to point out the value that some things have independently of an impartial, universal view. In this case it is a value that is conditioned on a lack of impartiality". J.Glass*

5. *"Imagine we have a large family and one miserable middle*

child. Should we not therefore eliminate one miserable child and conceive a happier one?" Dale Jamieson

6. "If we can prevent something bad without sacrificing anything of comparable significance, we ought to do it; absolute poverty is bad; there is some poverty we can prevent without sacrificing anything of comparable moral significance; therefore we ought to prevent some absolute poverty". Peter Singer

7. "Singer's works, remarkably for a philosophy professor, contain little or no philosophical argument. They derive their radical moral conclusions from a vacuous utilitarianism that counts the pain and pleasure of all living things as equally significant and that ignores just about everything that has been said in our philosophical tradition about the real distinction between persons and animals". Roger Scruton.

8. "Singer's rarefied rationalism of almost total impartiality is thus impossible to live out and fails his basic test of the practicality of ethics". Gordon Preece

9. "Above all, we must at all times remember that people matter more than concepts and must come first. The worst of all tyrannies is the heartless tyranny of ideas". Paul Johnson

Situation Ethics

Joseph Fletcher's Situation Ethics (1966) was written against a cultural background of rebellion against rules and values which limited individual choice. His theory has two targets - **LEGALISM**, the love of law, and **ANTINOMIANISM**, the belief that all rules are wrong. "We would be better advised to drop the legalist's love of law and adopt the law of love", he writes (SE page 74).

Fletcher's theory is firmly in a liberal Christian tradition which places the supreme value on human choice. He refers, for example, to the theologian Emile Brunner, and the German martyr to Hitler, Dietrich Bonhoeffer to illustrate how laws cannot be absolute, but only relative to the situation. He quotes Brunner approvingly: "None of the commandments in the Sermon on the Mount are to be understood as laws"[11], only the general principle "do to others as you would have them do to you" (Matthew 7.13).

Pastor Dietrich Bonhoeffer's action in joining the Stauffenburg bomb plot, as depicted in the film Valkyrie, is also described as a model example of situational ethics - he decides to suspend the law of "thou shalt not kill" when it is most loving to do so, in order to save many deaths.

Fletcher's argument goes like this:

1. All laws have exceptions.

2. The exceptions are determined by the situation.

---

11 The Divine Imperative page 136, quoted on page 77.

3. In every situation we must consider consequences.

4. Therefore all absolute laws are in fact relative to the situation.

We must therefore "relativise the absolute" (SE page 75), where the absolute is the rule or law. But we cannot "absolutise the relative" as **UNIVERSAL NORMS** are still important as foundations for ethics.

THE CASE AGAINST LEGALISM

Legalism involves directives which must be obeyed irrespective of the situation. Fletcher argues that Judaism, Catholicism and Protestantism have all been legalistic, and the legalism has bred immoral attitudes and outcomes.

Judaism is based on a legal code of 613 precepts developed from the Torah[12], the first five books of the Bible. A complex process of interpretation, providing exceptions to the rules, was developed by rabbis called pilpul - a form of hair-splitting to allow certain exceptions. As the exceptions multiplied, according to Fletcher, Judaism lost sight of the prophetic tradition which "sensitively sought an understanding of the situation" (SE page 19).

Catholicism has developed its own code of rules based on **NATURAL LAW**. Natural law, derived from the idea of the ideal rational purpose of human beings, has been repudiated by Paul's insistence, argues Fletcher, that "what matters is not what is legal but what is upbuilding" (SE page 75). Moreover there is even doubt about what the agreed principles of the natural law, the primary precepts, might be. According to Fletcher "there are no "universal laws" held by all men everywhere at all times" (SE page 76), so natural law is a "bad fix" and a "quicksand". Recall that the denial of universals is one of the preconditions of moral **RELATIVISM**. However, we need to be careful here: there are no universal laws, but there is, Fletcher argues, one universal principle: love.

What of the Protestant Scriptural tradition? We face two problems here, according to Fletcher. The first is one of interpretation; what do verses

---

12 The Torah or Law comprises Genesis, Exodus, Leviticus, Deuteronomy and Numbers.

like "render unto Caesar things that are Caesar's" actually mean? And secondly, there is the problem of application - having worked out what it means, we have to apply the sayings and rules. The "puritanical insistence on moral rules" means "they have lost touch with the headaches and heartbreaks of life" (SE page 20). The anti-gay movement so prevalent in Protestant churches bears witness, says Fletcher, to the unloving and disastrous decisions of this form of legalism.

The conclusion is that both the naturalistic reason of natural law theory and the legalistic revelation of those who rely on "the Word of God" has bred unloving condemnation or worse, a distorted sense of values where "an adulterer is more wicked than a politician who takes bribes" (Bertrand Russell[13]). The ethics of law is responsible for much evil in the world. We need a new Christian ethic: situationism.

---

13 *Why I am not a Christian page 33, quoted by Fletcher 1966:20*

ANTINOMIANISM

Antinomianism (nomos = law) implies no maxims or rules at all. "In every 'existential moment' or 'unique situation, one must rely upon the situation itself, there and then, to provide the ethical solution" (SE page 22). Rather than gaining guidance from a moral maxim, antinomians follow a "built-in radarlike faculty" (SE page 23), which is "close to the intuition theory of conscience".

Fletcher gives a Christian example and an atheistic example of how antinomianism has developed. He again cites Paul to support his view that Gnostic anarchy threatened the foundations of Christianity. Paul spent some time in his first letter to the Corinthians (1 Cor 6: 12-20) arguing against the spirit-led special knowledge (gnosis in Greek) which had inspired a revival in Corinth, where prophets seem to reign unchecked whilst moral behaviour evaporated (drunkenness, orgies, incest were all cited by Paul).

Fletcher also applauds Sartre's honesty in developing **EXISTENTIALISM**, whilst at the same time seeing it as another example of atheistic antinomianism. One overarching coherence which we impose on reality is "bad faith" according to Sartre, and we should live with the basic incoherence of the world as a fact.

> *"There is no fabric or web of life, hence no basis for generalising moral principles or rules" (SE page 25).*

So we have to make our own way in "good faith" according to the existentialist, by defining who we are and who we want to be, unshackled by law, tradition or culture.

Clearly there are similarities between Sartre's view and Fletcher's such as the emphasis on freedom, courage and choice. However, Fletcher would not want situation ethics branded as a branch of existentialism, as it holds firmly to one moral absolute - agape love.

SITUATIONISM

Fletcher stresses that we inherit tradition of ethical values from our community and family. We "treat them with respect as illuminators of our problems", (SE page 26) but then prepare to set them aside "in the situation if love is better served". He quotes Bishop John Robinson, "situationism cannot but rely, in deep humility, upon guiding rules, upon the cumulative experience of one's own and other people's obedience"[14]. While accepting the reasonable basis for law, as in natural law theory, or the importance of divine revelation as in Protestant legalism, the situationist turns the categorical rules (with no exceptions), into hypothetical decisions. So (my example) "thou shalt not kill", becomes, "it is acceptable to kill if a mad gunman is threatening your child".

What determines the "if" here? What creates the hypothetical circumstance allowing us to break the rule? Fletcher's answer is "only love". "The situationist follows a moral law or violates it according to love's need" (SE page 26). **AGAPE** is the one universal rule or principle - to this extent Fletcher is an absolutist, not a relativist. However, situationism is relativistic in that every circumstance needs to be assessed on its own merits, according to the application of the rule of love. For this reason Richard Jacobs has described situation ethics, using Fletcher's own phrase (SE page 31) as "principled relativism"[15].

Fletcher sees this as a form of Christian ethics. He quotes Paul approvingly "for the whole law is fulfilled in one word, "you shall love your neighbour as yourself" (Gal 5:14). Jesus attacked the legalism of the Pharisees, and in being what Bonhoeffer calls "the man for others","is to be for others, for neighbours. That is agape" (SE page 80).

---

14 *Honest to God page 119-120 quoted in Fletcher page 32*

15 *Richard Jacobs, Situation Ethics, Villanova State University website*

Fletcher goes further and argues that Jesus' crucifixion is a perfect example of agape situationism. "If love is to be understood situationally, we must understand that Jesus' going to the cross was his role and vocation in his situation with his obligation as the Son of God" (SE page 62), as it involved doing what he could, sacrificially, in the situation Jesus found himself. Fletcher believes that the relativistic, situational nature of his ethics is also a better way of exalting the sovereignty of God - who judges our true motive of love and has given us the very highest requirement - to fulfil love and exercise loving judgement.

WHAT DOES LOVE MEAN?

The one universal principle In Fletcher's ethic is **AGAPE** love. This Greek word is the most oft-used word for love in the New Testament. It is a central characteristic of God, for "God is love". It forms one of the four loves of Greek philosophy: eros, creative and procreative love, philia, friendship love, storge, family love and agape usually described as "sacrificial love" for neighbour and stranger[16].

The paradigm story of sacrificial love, which Joseph Fletcher doesn't discuss, is the parable of the Good Samaritan told by Jesus in Luke 22. Here a Samaritan outsider, who had intermarried outside the Jewish faith and so become unsound and despised by other Jews, is the one who takes the risk of stopping by the man who had been beaten up and left for dead. He then bandages up his injuries, takes him to a local inn and even promises to pay the bill when he next passes that way. This Samaritan is the true neighbour who loves the wounded man "as himself".

Fletcher stresses that agape is an attitude, not a feeling. "Christian love is not desire. Agape is giving love - non-reciprocal, neighbour-regarding - "neighbour" meaning "everybody", even an enemy...it is an attitude, not a feeling" (SE page 79).

This agape love is both interventionist and courageous. Agape takes decisions, and a decision is "a risk rooted in the courage of being free" (SE page 84). Fletcher gives the example of Jesus eating corn on the Sabbath and justifying his action by the story of David, when he was hungry, who ate the bread of the Tabernacle "which it is lawful only for the priests to eat" (Luke 6:1-5). Again, this courage is close to what

---

16 For an excellent discussion of these see The Four Loves by C.S. Lewis

Sartre means by "good faith" - an existentialism of integrity and courage.

Fletcher acknowledges the similarity with utilitarianism. The greatest good of the greatest number calls for a calculation in the distribution of benefits, as "love and justice are the same". It is a demanding ethic based on equal concern for neighbour, stranger, enemy and friend. However, as we shall see, Fletcher argues that all value statements are faith statements rather than empirical statements provable true or false by their consequences, as the utilitarians argue.

FOUR WORKING PRINCIPLES

Pragmatism

Pragmatism gives situation ethics its method, not its end. The rightness of an action depends, however, on using this method - because rightness depends on success. "The good", argues Fletcher, "like the true, is whatever works"' (SE page 42). Quoting Wiliam James approvingly, Fletcher argues "pragmatism turns its back on bad a priori reasons, fixed principles, cLosed systems, and pretended absolutes..towards facts and actions and power" (SE page 43).

Any action is judged successful only in terms of one value: love.

Relativism

Fletcher describes his theory as **"PRINCIPLED RELATIVISM"** because although it has relativistic aspects, there is one absolute at its heart, love. We have become relativistic in the way we reason because our ways of thinking come out of our culture (just as situation ethics we might argue comes out of 1960s culture). Our ends, the things we pursue are relative to our desires and human desires change with the times.

Fletcher here is talking particularly about what we can call relativism of application. Everything the situationist does is evaluated against the one absolute norm of love. It does not "absolutise the relative" because if everything is relative, including the summum bonum or greatest good, we would fall, according to Fletcher, into antinomian anarchy.

Fletcher acknowledges his debt to Emil Brunner's Divine Imperative

(1932) and Roald Niebuhr's Moral Man and Immoral Society (1932). The divine command remains absolute, but "how to do it depends on our own responsible estimate of the situation" (SE page 45). I would argue this is a perfectly legitimate reading of Jesus' parable of the Good Samaritan, told in response to a question "and who is my neighbour?", and the application of the question "how do I love him or her?".

Finally, Fletcher justifies this relativism with reference to human creatureliness. He quotes Isaiah: "my ways are not your ways, says the Lord" (Isaiah 55:8). We are always seeking anew to grasp the unfathomable mysteries of God, in the meaning of agape love and also how agape love is best applied to our world of atom bombs, famine and capitalist excess. To pretend we can ever fix the meaning or the application is to misunderstand how truth always has a relativistic element.

Positivism

Relativism gives us the context, that values come from culture and situations, pragmatism the method, the case by case approach ("casuistry" is Fletcher's word for this case by case feature), and positivism explains how we arrive at the end or **TELOS** of agape love. Fletcher contrast the summum bonum (greatest good) of situation ethics with the end of natural law. Natural law invokes a naturalistic method of arriving at an end, as the end is defined by humankind's rational natural purposes or tendencies. These tend to be fixed and are explained as designed into us by God.

With "theological positivism" these truths are affirmed by faith, not by reason. We cannot prove that God is love, we assume it and accept it on trust. Love as an idea cannot be defined in terms of anything else, and the statement "love is the highest good" cannot be proved empirically.

Values are like beauty argues Fletcher. "Aesthetic and moral values are like faith propositions, they are based on choice and decision" (SE page 48). Like existentialist ethics, we have to make a leap of faith, with courage and commitment. "Love is good" is of the same order of statement as "this painting is good". "In Christian ethics the key category of love is established by deciding to say "yes" to the faith assertion "God is love"and then to the value assertion "love is the highest good" (SE page 49). The faith comes first, according to Fletcher. This makes Situation ethics a particularly Christian form of relativism as the commitment is to a God who is (we believe) love.

Fletcher's view that all values are faith values is contested by **NATURALISTS** (who see goodness as a natural, empirical feature for the world) like Alasdair MacIntyre, a virtue ethicist, or the utilitarians. To say we can't prove that love is good is to imply we cannot evaluate the good consequences of love - which is an empirical test, and surely one that anyone can do. Try loving all members of your family for one day in a sacrificial way and you should be able to notice an improvement in human welfare and happiness. This is all the naturalists claim. We might conclude that Fletcher doesn't need to argue from a positivistic faith stance - it is possible in principle to prove naturalistic goodness by pointing to good effects.

Personalism

The value of love is a means to an end where that end is individuals in need. So "situation ethics puts people at the centre of concern, not things" (SE page 50). Rather than being legalistic, situation ethics is personalistic. As Emil Brunner states, any values apart from people is "phantasmagoria"17. Any action is good only because it is good for someone. "Love is only extrinsically, never intrinsically valuable. Love is of people, by people, and for people" (SE page 51).

Fletcher is against Kant's **ABSOLUTISM**, but in favour of Kant in two respects. He approves of Kant's idea that ethics is about practical reason, about working things out in a personal way using our minds. And he approves of Kant's second maxim: always treat people not just as means, but always as ends in themselves. This is close to what Fletcher implies by "personalism". Actually, Fletcher misquotes Kant in the same way my students usually do, "treat people as ends, never as means", he says (SE page 53). This is definitely not what Kant is saying : we shouldn't merely treat people as means, but we can't help partly doing so: your reading this is a means to getting an A level, but just make sure you write politely to me when you do, treating me as a person, just like you. So treat me, not **just** as a means, but always, also, as a person in my own right.

---

17 Emil Brunner The Divine Imperative page 194

THE SIX PROPOSITIONS

PROPOSITION	IMPLICATION
1. There is only one intrinsic good, "love".	There are no laws or absolutes, only love which when applied can result in lying in one situation, and telling the truth in another. Love "relativises the absolute" by making everything relative to this one intrinsic good.
2. There is one ruling norm: love.	Agape is a living principle seeking a neighbour's best interest: we "follow law for love's sake, not love for law's sake".
3. Love and justice are the same.	Love and justice are the same thing. Justice is love distributed according to need. Justice is a calculation we make relative to circumstances to many neighbours, whether we know them or not. This involves making estimates and choices between people.
4. Love wills the neighbour's good whether we like him or not.	Love is about will, not feeling, a command of Christ, not an option for his followers, we obey for God's sake and love the unloveable, even including our enemies (Matt 5:43–8). A neighbour is anyone in need: love is disinterested, impartial,

PROPOSITION	IMPLICATION
5. Only the end justifies the means, nothing else.	Means are always relative to ends. Everything (war, violence, lying, cheating) needs to be considered in terms of costs and benefits, as in utilitarian ethics – except here the benefit is the neighbours' good. The means must be fitting (appropriate), "the necessary end sanctifies
6. Love's decisions are made situationally, not prescriptively.	As free agents we see the moral life as an adventure, where reason replaces rules. We make choices bravely. In the complexity of modern moral decisions, we need to face hard decisions, and "sin bravely" in assessing the situation and acting

WILLIAM BARCLAY'S CRITIQUE

In Ethics in a Permissive Society, William Barclay presents a detailed criticism of Situation Ethics. In all the situations Fletcher discusses we are faced with a "terrifying degree of freedom", argues Barclay. Like the Grand Inquisitor in The Brothers Karamazov, we are right to argue that people want security, not freedom in this sense. We need the security of clear guidelines (or rules).

Moreover, freedom only works according to Barclay where there is perfect love. "If there is no love, then freedom can become licence, freedom can become selfishness or even cruelty"[18]. Because our love is imperfect, we are, Barclay thinks, not yet ready for this sort of freedom. It is too demanding, too risky. Again, "we need a certain amount of law, being the sort of people we are". He thinks that if we were all saints, situation ethics would be the perfect ethics. But we aren't.

Barclay takes a very different view of human nature to Fletcher's. Where Fletcher assumes our judgment is developed enough to exercise the situational judgement, Barclay argues we are always developing from childhood onwards. We grow in **WISDOM** and knowledge. We need to develop habits which are good habits and so grow in wisdom and right judgment. This is a process.

There is a debate in ethics about whether anything can be wrong absolutely, in every situation. Barclay thinks there are examples. For example, it is never right to start someone on a series of experiments with recreational drugs that can lead to addiction and even death. To break up a family in the name of love, for example by having an affair,

---

18 ibid. page 81

can never be right. Genocide can never be right.

Finally, Barclay gives us five reasons why law, including moral rules, is good and beneficial.

1. Law is based on the wisdom and experience of society.

2. Law translates morals into social disciplines.

3. Law defines what is wrong.

4. Law discourages people from committing a moral wrong - it provides incentives to be good.

5. Law protects society - it has a social benefit.

To sum up: William Barclay does not share the situationist "phobia of the law". He rejects the oppositions set up between freedom and law in Fletcher's theory. "Freedom and law go hand in hand..by the influence of law people come in the end to be really free"[19], argues Barclay. Right at the end of his second book, Fletcher seems to agree with Barclay, that freedom only makes sense when we are perfectly good - that goodness comes before freedom : "until sin is no more"[20].

Maybe the problem with Situation Ethics may be its assumption about human nature: it assumes we are good enough, and wise enough, to take all decisions for ourselves, looking only at the situation.

---

19 ibid. page 89

20 Moral Responsibility page 94.

STRENGTHS AND WEAKNESSES

Strengths

- **PERSONAL** - Situation ethics takes the individual seriously, and the particular situation they face. So it is a compassionate ethics, looking at an individual's needs, interests and circumstances before it considers what ethical rules society would normally apply in this case. Then if love requires it, a situationist has the courage to break rules.

- **FLEXIBLE** - Situation ethics is a flexible ethics because it requires a case by case judgment. We are encouraged to use reason and to look and listen carefully to a person's needs. Laws have their rightful place as background wisdom, but the individual still needs to exercise flexible judgment. So as Christian ethic, we escape the absolutism of Natural Law theory, or the legalism of Protestant Bible-based Christianity. Christianity can at last assume a loving face.

- **JUST** - Situation Ethics has a strong idea of justice based on the individual and a fair treatment of their situation. This implies a fair distribution of benefits, but also a case by case approach to treating people. Equality does not mean an equal share - sometimes shares have to be unequal because someone's needs are greater. Love and justice are the same, argues Fletcher. Perhaps he was right.

Weaknesses

- **AGAPE IS TOO DEMANDING** - Fletcher's ethic places at its centre the one intrinsic good of love. The meaning of agape is "sacrificial love for the stranger" that even extends to our enemy. All of us, Christian or non-Christian, are supposed to follow this ethic. If I'm on the way to coffee with a friend, am I really supposed to drop my £10 in the hat of the homeless man sitting under the archway?

- **LAW IS USEFUL** - Joseph Fletcher admits there is a place for law, but we need to set it aside when love needs us to. But William Barclay argues, there is more to law than Fletcher admits. Law and freedom go together, because law defines (usually) what society at that moment agrees is wise and good. It is for society to debate and change the law, not for situationists to throw the law aside according to some instant judgment.

- **CALCULATION IS DIFFICULT** - as with all consequentialist ethics, Situation ethics asks us to make a calculation of the likely future consequences of our action. This is very demanding and requires a lot of experience of the world to get it right. Bishop John Robinson calls situation ethics "the only ethic of man come of age", but you would need to be very old to really make use of it, and by that time, you would have had a lifetime of mistakes and heartache to live with.

SELF-TEST: KEY TERMS

agape - consequentialism - positivism - personalism - pragmatism - relativism - legalism - working principles

SELF-TEST QUESTIONS

1. Outline Fletcher's four working principles.

2. What does Fletcher mean by saying "love relativises the absolute, it does not absolutise the relative"?

3. Fletcher calls his ethic "principled relativism". What does he mean by this?

4. How might these four principles apply to a young woman facing an abortion?

5. Is Fletcher correct to see love and law as opposites?

6. Holmes was the first mate of a ship that sank. In an overcrowded lifeboat he pitched all the males into the sea. "Situation ethics says it was bravely sinful, a good thing" (1966:136). Explain.

7. Evaluate William Barclay's view, that Fletcher underestimates the value of law.

8. Do the strengths of situation ethics outweigh the weaknesses?

9. Why might the parable of the Good Samaritan lead to the conclusion that Jesus was a situationist?

10. "Sometimes it is necessary to put principles aside and do the right thing". Fletcher quotes and describes the St Louis cabbie as the hero of his book. Why?

Conclusions

The teleological ethics discussed in this book are all consequentialist[21]. They identify an end by examining the rational desires of human beings, and then quantifying goodness by assessing how much a decision maximises that end. At the start of this book I suggested we adopt the DARM approach to examining ethical theories. This involves answering four questions:

- **DERIVATION** - how is goodness determined or derived by this theory?

- **APPLICATION** - how is goodness applied to a situation to give a "good action"?

- **REALISM** - does the theory give a realistic account of human nature and our own experience of moral decision making?

- **MOTIVATION** - how does the theory answer the question "why should I be moral"?

IS TELEOLOGICAL ETHICS RELATIVISTIC?

Before answering the four questions, it's important to say something about the issue which is often confusing: is teleological consequentialism relative or absolute? How are we to classify these theories? There are a number of meanings of relativism, and it is beyond the scope of this book to mention all of them. However, we have established that teleological

_____

21 It's worth stressing again that not all teleological theories are consequentialist - virtue ethics for example.

theories are relativistic in one meaning of the word, but also absolutist in another.

Teleological theories cannot have absolute rules that apply everywhere, always in any circumstance. Even Mill, whose theory is one of rule utilitarianism, doesn't argue that the rules we follow are hard and fast and always apply. They are not absolute. Teleological theories conclude instead that the moral good is always best maximised by examining the circumstances, and that sometimes it's good to lie, and sometimes it's not.

This conclusion comes from the very nature of teleological ethics, be it Situation Ethics or Utilitarianism. This is because the idea of what is good comes first. I first decide on my value of goodness. Then I decide how to act by applying that value. Let's call this a relativism of application.

Of course we have at least four candidates in this book for what is thought to be "good". Notice these aren't themselves moral values, there is nothing we would immediately say about pleasure for example that makes it good. Bentham argues it is good simply because we desire it, it is a fact of human nature, something given, something we just accept. The same applies to the other three candidates for the idea of goodness: happiness, preferences, or love.

The idea that connects this value of "goodness" which we connect to pleasure, happiness, preferences or love is consequences. It is the consequences or results of an action which define what is good, not my motive or anything else inherent in the action itself. If the consequences maximise the value for the most people, then that action is good. In this sense goodness is always relative to consequences, and to the situation.

However, teleological ethicists do claim one norm at the centre of their theories, even if they disagree about what that norm is. Love is different from happiness, and happiness is different from pleasure. Nonetheless, they all claim that these things are intrinsically good, they are good in themselves. Of course, making a claim isn't the same as proving the case: Mill's proof of utilitarianism is the weakest part of his essay. He ends up arguing that happiness is good because most people desire it.

It follows that on the level of values, rather than of application, teleological ethics is absolute. The principle of love in Joseph Fletcher's theory is something we commit to because we assent or agree that it is good. Fletcher's idea of positivism means just this: he is honest enough to say he can't prove agape love is the best value. It is nonetheless an absolute value (it applies everywhere and always), and so Fletcher calls his theory (and we could call utilitarianism as well) "principled relativism".

DERIVATION

Does teleological ethics tend towards a multilevel approach?

Utilitarian and situation ethics both derive goodness from a fact of human nature - the fact that we desire pleasure or happiness, or the fact that we choose to believe in the cause of love (Fletcher's positivism). So they are naturalistic theories, deriving what we ought to do from a state of affairs or fact in the natural world of experience.

Teleological consequentialist ethics, however, faces two particular problems: how do I accurately calculate consequences? Secondly there is the problem that society's interests don't necessarily correspond to my own interests. Think, for example, of speed limits - it is in society's interest to enforce speed limits but in my own interest (especially if I'm late for work) to break them.

All three utilitarian theories have tried to get round these problems by adopting a multilevel approach (my term). Even Bentham , who would appear to be the most individualistic, has a form of multilevel calculation. At Level 1, I calculate my utility involved in an action, and then, level 2 estimate everyone else's pleasure and pain. Bentham, remember, is very strong on equality - everyone's interests are to count equally. In the speeding example, social utility of keeping the limit (less noise, increased safety) exceeds personal utility, so I should therefore avoid speeding.

Mill is a weak rule utilitarian. This implies, at level 1, that generally we should keep rules that experience has shown increase the general happiness, rules such as telling the truth, keeping promises, not abusing people, and keeping the speed limit. But what happens when two "goods" come into conflict? For example, I am asked to tell a lie to cover for a friend who has bunked off school to go to a football match? Here truth-telling and loyalty to my friend are in conflict. Then, says Mill, we revert to being an act utilitarian and weigh up the consequences in this particular case. It would be right, in Mill's own example, to kidnap a reluctant surgeon and force him to operate on a dying friend. We can call this a level 2 calculation - we assess the utility of an individual act.

Singer's two levels operate slightly differently. He is a preference utilitarian, but faces the problem that we can't assess the preferences of persons who can't communicate with us. Preferences can only be stated by conscious, feeling, communicating beings. As argued in a previous chapter, Singer comes up with two levels of personhood, the conscious, rational person, aware of past and future, and the feeling but non-rational one, with no awareness of personal identity. He calls the second sort "entities". So at level 1, Singer asks us to assess the consequences of an action in terms of what most persons (not entities) prefer.

But what of feeling entities who can't communicate? Here, at level 2, we make an act utilitarian assessment. We try to assess what would be the least painful option for them and for society. This means, for example, with a severely disabled baby, we can argue that the baby's suffering will be lessened if the child is killed, and then, social happiness would be increased by replacing the child with a happier one. As we have seen, there are assumptions we have to make about the baby who is disabled, such as what conscious life they have, what their prospects are for a happy life. The problem of calculation never entirely disappears with utilitarian ethics, and has led some to argue that we are imposing our own views about such things on "entities" who are unable to speak for themselves.

APPLICATION

Does the end justify the means?

In applying the good of maximising happiness or pleasure utilitarian ethics and situationism both stand accused of creating immoral outcomes, or outcomes which none of us would desire when faced with a similar choice.

A central problem with teleological ethics is that it says, with Joseph Fletcher, "that the end always justifies the means". This seems to go against our moral intuition. If the end always justifies the means, then if it would cause a terror suspect to tell me where a bomb is hidden, it would be morally right to torture and kill his children in front of him. Or, as Joseph Fletcher recounts, if it is necessary to throw ten men out of an overcrowded lifeboat against their will in order to give the women and children a better chance of survival, I should do so.

Bernard Williams calls this the problem of integrity. A utilitarian might say it's the right thing to do to kill an innocent child, but I couldn't force myself to do it. It destroys my integrity as a human being, someone with beliefs, values and virtues. Mill would agree: he argued that virtues such as integrity and honesty were good in themselves because in attaining them we find happiness. Maintaining my integrity intact would, according to Mill, be entirely consistent with utilitarian ethics. Mill would never have accepted the invitation, in Bernard Williams own example, to shoot the indian. The general loss of integrity if everyone behaved like this would cause such misery that the utilitarian calculation would always cause us to decline the offer to kill.

Does utilitarian ethics and situation suffer from the difficulty, that it seems to go against our intuitions of what is moral? Does this matter? Should we reject utilitarianism for this reason our alter our intuitions?

REALISM

Is teleological ethics unrealistic?

Utilitarian ethics is demanding in two senses. As we have seen, it demands that I make a calculation of future happiness which I may not be wise or knowledgeable enough to make. And secondly, it expects me to make sacrifices for the greater good which I may be unwilling to make.

For example, if it would increase the happiness of poor people if I gave away 30% of my income, I should do this even if it means my son has to forego his new computer. If I am walking down the beach and I see a young girl struggling against a rip tide, I should go in and try to save her even if I am a weak swimmer and risk losing my life. I should even, if faced with a choice between saving my son and a nuclear physicist in a house fire, save the nuclear physicist first on the grounds that she will contribute more in future happiness than my son.

Does this make utilitarian ethics unrealistic in what it demands of me? Arguably utilitarianism fails to account for two things: partiality, that I quite reasonably give greater weight to my own children than I do to a stranger, and lack of foresight. I just don't know what the consequences of my action will be and so I can't begin to judge , on the basis of two choices, which one will have the greatest utilitarian value.

MOTIVATION

Why should I be moral?

To be moral implies that I care enough to apply some value of goodness to people around me, or even to strangers I may never meet. Bentham presents this as a psychological fact. But why should I care about a stranger? Bentham argues we are all by nature pleasure-seekers who desire pleasure, not pain. So pleasure is good, and pain is bad. I can understand why this applies to me, but if I go no further, this seems to be simply a form of egoism. Does Bentham establish a case for why I should care for others? In fact Bentham is at pains to stress that we don't naturally care about others: in his "Remarks on Bentham's Philosophy" (1833), Mill quotes Bentham's The Book of Fallacies that "in every human breast… self-regarding interest is predominant over social interest; each person's own individual interest over the interests of all other persons taken together."

Bentham would have been horrified to be branded a selfish egoist. He gives three reasons why we should care about others. Bentham believed all moral theories (following David Hume) can be "reduced to the principles of sympathy and antipathy," which are the feelings that describe utility. Secondly, he argues that pleasure is good irrespective of whether it's my pleasure or the pleasure of a stranger - we are all equal. So, like Singer, Bentham argues we should look at people's desires and interests in a neutral way, taking away whose interests exactly we are talking about. Thirdly, Bentham saw it as the role of a Parliament to do just this - to look at everyone's interests and pleasure/pain in a disinterested way. He asks us in way to look at his morality and agree that this is the best way to resolve disputes and generate a world which is happier and better for all of us.

Mill was also aware of this problem and, building on Bentham, seems to bring in the virtue of sympathy to explain why I care. I am capable, by a leap of imagination of sympathising with those I have never even met, and so sacrificing my interests and happiness for theirs. So I jump into the swollen stream to save a drowning child because I sympathise with them as a fellow human (feeling) being. Mill differs from Bentham, though, in that he sees virtues as essential to happiness. He believes you and I are motivated by more than pleasure, that virtues that build character are also things that are recognised as good in themselves and so we will think them worth pursuing.

Fletcher argues not so much for a fact of human nature (that I naturally sympathise and see the value of virtues like self-sacrifice), but from the fact of conversion. Approving of Kant's second formula of the categorical imperative, that we should always treat people as not just means to an end, but as ends in themselves, Fletcher argues that I acknowledge, by agape love, that everyone has equal rights and interests. The individual matters. My motivation for doing loving things is, at the end of the day, because I believe in love; I have assented to join the great cause of creating a more loving world. Fletcher knows we cannot prove the beauty of this cause, but we can understand it and agree to join it.

What of Peter Singer? Like other utilitarians, he urges us to adopt the universal viewpoint, to consider my own interests as no better or more significant than anyone else's. He combines this with a view of personhood that excludes some people we classify as persons (babies up to four weeks old, the severely disabled, those on life-support machines in a persistent vegetative state) and includes other beings we would not normally include as persons (such as apes, monkeys, gorillas). Is Singer asking too much of us to step out from our normal feelings and loyalties and give substantial proportions of our incomes to the poor, and also kill those who appear to have no sense of a past or future? Is this moral empiricism going much too far, into a cold, dark place where, courageously, but misguidedly, it exhorts us to do things we just could never face doing?

References

- **BARCLAY, W.** - Ethics in a Permissive Society, Harper Collins, 1972

- **BENTHAM, J.** - An Introduction to the Principles of Morals and Legislation. Oxford: Clarendon Press, 1996.

- **CRISP, R.** - Routledge Philosophy Guidebook to Mill on Utilitarianism, 104.

- **FLETCHER, J.** - Situation Ethics, 1966.

- **MILL, J.S.** - Utilitarianism, Hackett Publishing, 2002

- **POJMAN, L.** - Ethics, Discovering Right and Wrong, Wadsworth, 2001.

- **SINGER, P.** - Practical Ethics, Cambridge , 1994

- **SMART, JJC.** - "An Outline of a System of Utilitarian Ethics," in

- **SMART, JJC** and **WILLIAMS, B**. - Utilitarianism: For and Against, by,

- eds.

Postscript

Peter Baron taught Religious Studies at Wells Cathedral School from 2006-12, and before that taught Economics and Politics at Tonbridge School in Kent (1982-1991). He currently works as a freelance speaker and writer and is producing a series of books on ethics to be published in 2013.

This revision guide is based on detailed handouts and powerpoints on the author's website. A teacher's guide is being prepared with detailed powerpoints, games, templates, and activities. Please consult the website for further details.

Students seeking fuller explanations and a bibliography should also consult the website which also contains exam tips and past questions listed by theme.

The author welcomes comments on the Revision Guide and contributions to the website - details are to be found online at:

www.philosophicalinvestigations.co.uk